welcome

Good things come in small packages. That often-heard missive applies to the 45 baths featured in this book. Simply put, *Better Homes and Gardens*® *Small Bath Solutions* celebrates smallness—and the clever approaches homeowners and designers have taken to shower their grooming spaces and powder rooms with style and function.

What constitutes a small bath? That depends on your vantage point. A small bath in a Midwestern home might seem like a pampering paradise in a New York City apartment, where one can often spread arms and touch walls on both sides. Our featured rooms run the gamut from pint-size to modestly sized. The commonality is that they've done a lot with a little. Let the photographs and stories inspire your own ideas for finagling a tight floor plan and embracing style. The Bath Workbook section at the back of this book will help you narrow down choices in tile, countertops, and more. Whether you're in the dreaming or doing stage of a renovation, remember that dimensions are only numbers. Even in a small bath, the sky is the limit.

contents

compact
creativity

1

Amazing things happen when you embrace the possibilities. Imagine a seldom-used tub removed to allow space for a walk-in shower. Consider how a "floating" vanity could give your bath much-needed breathing room, or how a niche built between studs in the wall could eke out an extra bit of storage. The baths on the following pages incorporate those design-smart features and more. They're glass-half-full kinds of spaces.

Getting your bath to reach its full potential starts by looking beyond what it is to what it could be. Rank your priorities, and let the ones that float to the top guide your makeover. Be prepared for compromises. For example, if you discover that your space simply can't accommodate a double-sink vanity, consider a wide single sink that can offer two-person functionality when needed. Remember, it's not the size of the room that matters, but what you do with it. Even in a small bath, you can do a lot.

open and accommodating

Space-stretching solutions and fresh updates fill this bath with function and Florida-vacation spirit.

Brown linoleum and worn-out laminate prompted Deborah and Bob Jones to gut the guest bath in their Florida getaway home.

Inspired by the beach and water nearby, Deborah created a new look for the space, choosing design elements that convey the couple's carefree, sand-on-the-floor vacation lifestyle. At the same time, she improved the bath's efficiency for their children and guests.

The most dramatic change came from removing soffits above the sink and old tub-and-shower combo. "Raising up the ceiling changed the whole feel of the room," Deborah says. "I was able to get more light and build the cabinets a little higher." The tub gave way to a walk-in shower with a bench. "It's more fun, more open, and a little bit more practical to get in and out of," Deborah says.

LEFT: Glass tiles in oceany hues extend around the room, while quartz surfacing on the counter suggests beach sand. OPPOSITE: A walk-in shower and colorful glass tile create a light, inviting guest bath.

A partial wall separates the shower from the toilet, while a clear door shows off glass wall tiles. "By running the tiles across the wall, behind the toilet, and into the shower, it expanded the whole feeling," says interior designer Dorothy Mainella, a member of the National Kitchen & Bath Association (NKBA).

When the bath is not being used by the couple's children, it serves overnight visitors. To provide more space for guests' toiletries, Deborah boosted storage in the vanity area. There's plenty of counter space around the sink, and upper cabinets topped by open shelves flank the mirror. A cutout in the base cabinetry keeps the vanity from appearing boxy and heavy.

A soft color scheme adds to the lighter look. The glass wall tiles, in oceany shades of blue, green, and gray, set the tone, contrasting gently with the crisp white cabinetry. The quartz-surfacing countertop and tan floor tile mimic the look of wet sand. A louvered entry door conveys casual Key West style.

"I think the room wanted a cottage, beachy feel that represents the water and sand we're so close to," Deborah says.

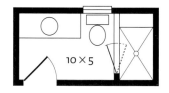

10 × 5

ABOVE: **Glass-front cabinets evoke the look of windows, fostering an open, breezy feel.** OPPOSITE: **The vanity offers several storage options, including a center bar for towels. Lighting below upper cabinets illuminates the counter. A louvered entry door sets a casual tone for the room.**

squared off

There's no longer a showdown over who gets to use what first in this clean-lined space.

The morning rush can be tough in a tight-fit bath.
Two people trying to shower and groom in about a 5-foot square—and get out the door in time for work—isn't exactly a Zen way to start the day. But it was reality for Michigan homeowners Todd McLaughlin and Roger Nickels.

Finally having had enough of jockeying for a spot in front of the mirror, they tapped bath designer Tanya Woods to redo the room. What she achieved was impressive. Working within the same sliver of space, Woods packed the bath with function and style—and gave the homeowners more than they imagined. The first order of business? Ditch the old blue tub that stretched wall to wall. Having it out of the room went a long way

LEFT: **Mosaic tiles on the floor continue into the shower, stretching the sight line onward and upward. They also provide visual relief from the large tiles on the walls.** OPPOSITE: **With limited wall space, the towel bar found a nifty home on the bottom of the horizontal cabinet.**

in visually opening the room. And having a new walk-in shower instead of a climb-into-it tub went a long way in ease, fitting the couple's on-the-go lifestyle.

The bulky old vanity with a Formica counter was another eyesore that got the heave-ho. In its place is a modern, open vanity that incorporates a shelf for towels and is topped with a wide sink. The homeowners knew that the double sink they hoped for was a long shot in the small space. Woods gave them the next best thing, bringing in a wider-than-usual sink that still allows two people to use it at the same time, if needed.

Similar good sense plays out above the vanity. A clean-lined cabinet stretches horizontally from the medicine chest. Though it provides extra storage, the bigger bonus is its sliding mirrored door that offers a secondary grooming spot. A towel bar mounted to the bottom of the cabinet was Woods' simple solution to dealing with a lack of wall space and also freeing up sight lines.

Improved function, however, is just half of it. The other half of the design equation is the room's newfound style. Rich wood and porcelain and glass tiles in earthy hues warm the space, which has a contemporary edge to it. "This is an older bungalow but it's transitional and on trend, so I wanted the bath to reflect that," Woods says. With tile covering the floor, vanity wall, and virtually all planes in the shower, the formerly dowdy room is now a spa-inspired escape.

"It's fantastic to use every day," Roger says, with Todd concurring. "Everything about the room works wonderfully—and looks wonderful, too."

Room for Improvement

Consider these tips before you launch into a makeover.

STRATEGY SESSION Put your money into a focal-point wall—usually the one that is first seen upon entering the room. In this bath, it's the vanity wall. Save even more by just tiling the backsplash.

VALUE VIEWPOINT Don't overdo. Though a renovated bath increases the value of a home, that doesn't mean going crazy. If you spend too much, you risk losing money when you sell.

EXTRA, EXTRA Make sure your budget has a cushion to accommodate unexpected extras that tend to crop up during a renovation. Allot extra when ordering materials, too. One builder suggests ordering 5 to 10 percent more flooring than you think you need. And hold on to scraps. You never know when you'll need another little piece of tile or molding, perhaps to frame out a mirror.

STAGE WORTHY If you can't afford your entire dream bath up front, do it in stages. Start with the more permanent elements, such as flooring and the shower or tub. You can swap out things like a sink, a faucet, a vanity, or a toilet later without disrupting the room.

ABOVE LEFT: The faucet throws a curve into the room's linear features, including the rectangular sink and square wall tiles. ABOVE: A partial, rather than full, wall and glass-block window keep the narrow shower from seeming claustrophobic. OPPOSITE: The extra-deep medicine chest and adjoining cabinet maximize storage space.

moving up

With access to a rooftop deck and a storage-packed hallway, this classic master bath offers so much more than grooming.

Atop winding stairs in Catherine Coquillard's 1939 home, there once was a den with a curious cubbyhole tucked behind. The previous owner had used the space for sewing, but Catherine barely used it at all—until she converted the den into a master bedroom and made the sewing room part of a sunny master bath.

Like many homes its age, the 2½-story stucco house in Oakland, California, didn't have a master suite, but the top floor seemed perfect for the role, given its access to a rooftop deck with treetop views. "The joy of this space is that it has completely unobstructed sun," Catherine says. "And it's very private. No one can see me, and I can't see anyone else."

Eager to exploit the views and the privacy, Catherine included a skylit shower and a toilet compartment on her bath wish list. "I knew other people might use the bath as a passage to the deck,

OPPOSITE: Crisp white cabinets with glass knobs spread the traditional charm of the 1939 home to the new master bath. Casement windows open onto a private deck. LEFT: A hallway that leads to the bath is now a tidy dressing area outfitted with built-ins.

so it was very important for the toilet to be separate," she says. Absent from her list was a whirlpool tub. "I'm not a tub person," Catherine says. "I already had a tub and a separate shower in the bath downstairs, and I never used the tub."

The challenge of making wishes reality fell to architect Bethany Opalach. "The design came down to inches—and sometimes to the half inch," Opalach says. The old sewing room couldn't hold every luxury, so Opalach stretched it by stealing a 6××10-foot space from the rooftop deck and using it to build a modest addition.

Entry to the new bath is through a dressing area with built-ins on one side and a small walk-in closet on the other. Directly ahead, sunlight streams through tall casement windows into the main bath. Its classic decor suits the home's 1930s roots, marrying crisply painted woodwork with pale carrara marble. "My house is very traditional," Catherine says. "It looks like someone's grandpa's house. I wanted the bath to match."

Though packed with space-efficient storage, the bath still feels airy, thanks to generous use of glass. "The windows, the skylight, the frameless shower enclosure, the mirror, the glass-front cabinet—they all help open up the space," Opalach says.

To complete the makeover, Opalach put a new deck over the existing rooftop surface. Because the deck sits higher than the bathroom floor, actual doors weren't practical, so the casement windows, resembling French doors, lead outside.

The setup doesn't hamper access. The outdoor space is one of the luxuries of the home. "The best thing is to get a cup of coffee and go out on the deck and read the paper in the morning," Catherine says.

"But I've even had cocktail parties out there. It's a wonderful place to sit in the sun and sip margaritas."

The shower, with its skylight and big windows, is almost as sunny. And with a natural veil of oak leaves fluttering just outside, it's equally private. "It's like being in a tree house," Catherine says.

ABOVE: The bath flows into a hallway that features a built-in dresser and shoe rack on one side and a walk-in closet on the other. The built-ins maximize storage without crowding the small space. Recessed, flat-panel cabinetry is used in both spaces for continuity.

1. INSIDE OUT

With a clear-glass wall and door, high windows with a view of trees, and a sun-catching skylight, the walk-in shower evokes the sensation of alfresco bathing. Large marble tiles cover the shower walls, while small versions pattern the floor.

2. PAMPERING SHOWER

A second showerhead—this one an adjustable-height model with handheld capability—lets the enclosure serve two people. A built-in niche holds accessories. Marble trim around the window opening and mildew-resistant paint on the wood sashes limit water worries.

3. LAUNDRY SMARTS

This pullout hamper, similar in design to a kitchen trash or recycling bin, includes a removable canvas liner for deft handling of laundry loads.

4. EASY-ACCESS STORAGE

Another kitchen-style pullout makes bath items stored under the sink easier to access.

master peace

A gift of Japanese art inspires the soothing redesign of a world-traveling couple's bath.

Sheer necessity drove Helen and Richard Podolske to remodel the upper-level bath of their home in Chevy Chase, Maryland. The shower leaked water into the ceiling below, the toilet never seemed to stop running, and the pink tiles stubbornly refused to match any paint colors found in stores.

The couple turned to designer Eugene Zagoskin, a member of the National Kitchen & Bath Association (NKBA), who had already redone the home's basement.

It didn't take long to hit on the perfect design inspiration: a print featuring the work of Kitagawa Utamaro, a Japanese artist from the late 1700s famous for his woodblock prints. The piece was a gift from a friend who knew how the globe-trotting couple loved Japan. They'd been looking for a place to display it, and the new bath would be perfect.

Helen says Japan is a place where she immediately felt at peace, so Zagoskin worked to bring that same sense of

RIGHT: Sconces flanking the mirror resemble bamboo, while tiny shelves display world-travel keepsakes. OPPOSITE: The frosted-glass door to this master bath suggests a shoji screen, signaling Asian influence within. It also helps the small room from seeming too closed in.

tranquillity into the bath, taking design cues from the print, which depicts an Asian woman clothed in red and gold.

The maple cabinetry is stained a Chinese red, while the marble countertop includes hints of gold. Clean lines throughout the bath also echo the print, as do natural-look materials. "The Japanese are open to nature," Zagoskin says.

The small bath also feels soothing because Zagoskin worked hard to make it seem larger. The shower, for example, features a clear-glass door, which extends the sight line and creates a sense of spaciousness. Frosted-glass cabinet doors

achieve a similar effect while partially obscuring everyday bath items stored within. "They give depth," Zagoskin says.

The bath is so captivating that a friend of the couple asked Zagoskin to make her one just like it. Imitation may be the sincerest form of flattery, but like the work of art that inspired it, this bath is one-of-a-kind.

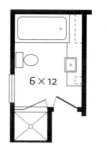

6 × 12

BELOW LEFT: The tub's thermostatic filler fits the clean-lined look of the room and ensures comfortable bathing. BELOW: Porcelain tiles in the shower were cut to odd sizes to create the look of a stone wall. OPPOSITE: The vanity countertop dovetails with the whirlpool tub to maximize display and storage space in the small bath. Wall-mount fixtures are another space-saving feature. The Japanese print that inspired the decor is reflected in the mirror.

smart growth

A couple shrewdly invest a small cache of space to yield big returns in their master bath.

With little space to spare in their Cincinnati home, Jo and Alan Henning faced a tough choice. They could either enlarge their compact master bath at the expense of their children's adjacent bath or find less-invasive ways to stretch their space. They chose the latter. "With four kids, we didn't think it was fair to give them a small bathroom so ours could be larger," Jo says.

Annexing a closet and a narrow slice of the kids' bathroom allowed Jo and Alan to add new amenities, including a much-desired second sink and their own tub. They also updated surfaces. Interior designer Andrea Stewart and bathroom designer Karen Bieszczak used clean lines and natural materials throughout the room to bring sophisticated style and a sense of spaciousness.

OPPOSITE: **A shallow vanity and a wide mirror are two of the design tricks that help this master bath feel more spacious and function better for the couple who use it.**

Rich cherry cabinetry introduces furniture style, while tumbled-limestone tiles on the floor, vanity countertop, and walls create design unity. The luxe materials are about more than good looks, though. They deftly disguise space-saving design strategies.

One case in point is the ledgelike vanity countertop. It's just 12 inches deep to give the couple better access to the toilet and shower, which occupy former closet space. The two sinks—a luxury in a small bath— are partially recessed into the countertop, their bowls projecting in cantilevered fashion.

Cabinets below the countertop are just deep enough to hold necessities. Two cubbies in the center of the vanity provide out-in-the-open storage for easy access to hand towels and grooming supplies. Bieszczak eked out additional storage by mounting a tall cabinet above the tub.

A ribbon of pretty pebbles embedded in the backsplash tile ties together the tidy design. "In my dreams, I live in a mountain cabin and bathe in a clear river," Jo says. "The pebbles bring that dream a bit closer to my current reality of a suburban existence."

Friendly Takeover

GIVE AND TAKE Space borrowed from an adjacent walk-in closet and bath enabled the master bath to grow from 7×8 feet to 9×14 feet, providing the square footage needed to add a tub and a second sink.

CHEAT SPACE The shallowness of the vanity area, with projecting sink bowls, allows easy access to the annexed space, where the toilet and shower were placed.

BE STRATEGIC The tub was placed along the exterior wall—where there's a window. That led to moving the door from the bedroom to a more central location, where it still opens straight to the vanity.

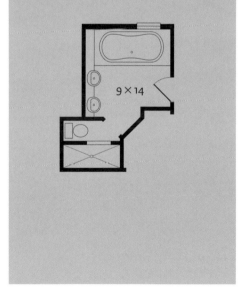

9 × 14

ABOVE RIGHT: **Cantilevered sinks keep the vanity slim and trim. A mosaic of pebbles adds color and whimsy.** OPPOSITE: **The homeowners added a tub to the once shower-only bath, conserving space by connecting the vanity to the tub with a tiled ledge.**

A shallow vanity—just 12 inches deep—frees up space without sacrificing style or storage.

seashell personality

A vanity dressed in nature's jewelry—shells and sand—establishes a fun focal point in a poolside bath that begged for a style splash.

THIS PHOTO: **An ordinary vanity becomes an artistic focal point with the addition of seashells, sand, and sea glass.** OPPOSITE: **A large clamshell functions as a thematic soap dish.**

After a fun day of splashing in the swimming pool, guests can use this St. Louis home's bathroom as a peaceful respite for showering and toweling off. White subway tile and a clear glass sliding enclosure for the shower combine with white beaded board on the surrounding walls to establish a tranquil setting.

The next step was to give the bath a visual connection to the poolside location. Customizing the vanity came to light as an affordable and clever possibility. For starters, pulls shaped like a starfish and a fish lend playful charm to the traditionally styled cabinet doors. Seashells embedded in sanded grout make the extra-deep retrofitted countertop a three-dimensional focal point.

Installing a border of glass tiles around the sink provides a smooth surface for setting down toiletries or a glass of water. More tiles were sandblasted and embedded in the sandy border to mimic sea glass.

RIGHT: **Seashells and glass tiles re-create a sandy beach on the countertop.** BELOW: **Sea creature–shape pulls continue the theme to the stock vanity doors.** OPPOSITE: **White subway tiles in the shower give the bath a breezy, clean feel.**

Get the Look

FRAME IT UP To create a beach-inspired countertop similar to the one in this bath, start with a plywood top and sides for your vanity. Cut the opening for the sink. Prime the plywood so it won't absorb water from the grout; let dry. Lightly sand; wipe away residue with a tack cloth.

LAY THE TILE Position glass or ceramic mosaic tiles around the opening cut for the sink, embedding the tile in tile adhesive. Let dry as suggested by the manufacturer. Fill joints with grout.

ADHERE FOUND ITEMS Assemble a collection of seashells and sea glass in colors to complement the bathroom decor. Have a small amount of clean sand on hand. Plan to work quickly and with a helper. While your helper spreads a thick layer of sanded grout over a small section of the vanity top or side, use a spackling knife to coat the backs of glass and shells (also fill shell cavities to avoid cracking). Press the shells and glass into the sanded grout, positioning the objects as desired. Have your helper apply more grout, if needed, and press more sand into the grout for an enhanced seashore effect. Continue working in sections to complete the top.

Featuring a floating base with generous drawers, open towel storage, and ample counter space, the long vanity embodies the clean, contemporary spirit of the bath. Custom-framed mirrors and a painting add artistic touches.

room to breathe

Sacrificing a seldom-used tub allowed these homeowners to gain eco-friendly elbow room.

Sometimes a bathroom needs a little breathing room. Such was the case in Bruce and Adrienne Staff's Boulder master bath. An imposing vanity and shower stall consumed one wall, making the room cramped, dark, and dreary—hardly the light-filled retreat the couple craved. "There just wasn't a feeling of spaciousness," Bruce says.

The couple teamed with interior designer Margie McCulloch to tap the room's hidden potential. That meant making some sacrifices. Because the Staffs rarely used the tub in the master bath, one of their first decisions was to replace the separate tub and shower with a spacious walk-in shower. The strategic move opened up the room to light and views while allowing a new dual vanity to have its own generous stretch of wall. "It turned a crowded, difficult-to-use space into a generous, user-friendly room," McCulloch says.

An ocean-inspired color scheme and a rich palette of eco-friendly materials infuse the room with a clean-lined, contemporary spirit. "The colors ground the room and add visual interest," McCulloch says. The various materials all come together at the vanity. There, rift-cut white oak forms the floating base cabinetry.

For eye-catching contrast, the vanity is topped with a black-flecked countertop made from recycled plastic bottles. And a mosaic backsplash formed from recycled-glass tiles frames the vanity in aqueous hues that sparkle in the sunlight.

The room's most unique feature stands between the dual sinks: a storage unit fashioned from kirei, a domestic agricultural product made of sorghum stock and elm. The open cabinet keeps towels at arm's reach, and its interesting texture adds energy to the horizontal lines of the vanity base. "We love the clean look of the vanity," Bruce says.

The vanity is strategically placed across from the shower, where a large window capitalizes on sunlit views. The abundance of natural light dances off the shower's interior—pale green ceramic field tile with a crackled finish and an ocean-hue tile border that matches the backsplash. Underfoot, limestone flooring installed in a running bond pattern spills out of the shower and across the room.

Radiant heat underneath the floor chases away the chill on cold days. Lighting beneath the vanity illuminates the tiles, providing a nifty feature. "When coming into the bathroom at night, you can light up the floors to clearly see where you're going and have no light in your eyes," McCulloch says.

The Staffs love the spacious, open atmosphere of their rejuvenated bath. "It's very bright and open for a not-so-big space," Bruce says. "It feels good to walk in there every day."

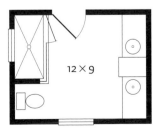

12 × 9

TOP LEFT: **The ocean hues of the glass-tile backsplash provide contrast against smooth black countertops.** TOP RIGHT: **A handheld showerhead teams with a fixed head on the opposite wall.** ABOVE: **The towel cabinet divides the dual sinks and adds a sense of movement.** ABOVE RIGHT: **Shower niche shelves of the same material as the vanity countertop provide storage convenience.** OPPOSITE: **The glass shower enclosure allows sunlight to spread throughout the room.**

space exploration

Rethink and rearrange. With those two words driving their remodeling project, these homeowners find a way to work in everything they need.

People rearrange their bedrooms when they need a change of pace, so why not take that concept to the bath? These homeowners did just that in their shift-things-around makeover. Though not as easily done as moving a bed or a dresser to a new wall, moving the fixtures opened up new possibilities for this room, and ultimately the people who use it.

To make the most of the floor space, the owners relocated the toilet to a new wall, below a window. This freed up a corner for a walk-in shower. Downsizing the tub ensured that pampering soaks wouldn't be a thing of the past. A petite claw-foot model sits next to the corner shower.

Clever little touches also contribute to the room's improved functionality. Though there's still just a single sink, it's an elongated version typically used in kitchens. The extra width means that two people can be brushing teeth side by side. On each side of the sink, corner-fit medicine cabinets are equipped with electrical outlets to keep small appliances handy, yet out of sight. And, blanketed in pale colors, the tidy bath is now a soothing retreat. More importantly, it's a room that finally makes sense of its space.

RIGHT: **An elongated sink typically used in kitchens is a clever way to gain more sink space. Open shelves below the sink provide extra storage. A tall vanity mirror reflects additional light. White window treatments (shown in the mirror's reflection) blend with the walls for a seamless appearance.**

ABOVE: **A 4-foot-long claw-foot tubs fits perfectly along a wall where the entry door swings open and also is clear of the corner shower entrance.** OPPOSITE TOP, LEFT: **One of the partial walls that encloses the shower provides privacy in the toilet area.** OPPOSITE TOP, RIGHT: **Covering the shower with the same tile used on the wall and keeping the entrance open makes it appear less intrusive.** OPPOSITE BOTTOM: **Small-pattern, tone-on-tone tiles create the illusion of spaciousness.**

Elongating sight lines makes a small space seem larger. Because this claw-foot tub is open underneath, it appears to take up less space than the old built-in model.

Function First

Daunting as it may seem, it is possible to make a small bath more functional. Take inspiration from this bath's space-enhancing shifts.

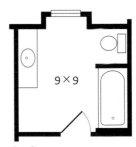

before

IN THE SWING Changing the direction the door swings opened up an unused corner for cabinetry.

STORAGE MINDED Centering the sink on one wall and flanking it with cabinetry provided enough storage for multiple users.

ON THE MOVE Moving the toilet under the window provided the square footage needed for a custom-tiled corner shower. Replacing the built-in tub with a small claw-foot model increased sight lines.

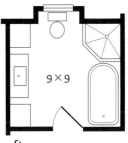

after

complete recovery

Space-expanding design and a tongue-in-cheek medical theme give this bath a big shot in the arm.

THIS PHOTO: **A vintage steel hospital cabinet came from a supply house that provides period pieces for films.** OPPOSITE: **The big red cross on the shower curtain sets the tone for this medically minded bath.**

Some baths are pretentious, but not this one in Jay and Bryna Kranzler's San Diego home. Inspired by Jay's medical career, it injects serious function with a dose of hospital humor.

"On the one hand, the design is consistent with the gravity and sterility of the old hospital/apothecary setting upon which it is modeled," Jay says. "On the other hand, the severity of the setting is tempered with the recognition that bathrooms can be funny, especially to teenage boys like my two sons, who share the bathroom."

Tweaking existing space in the modest-size bath healed a fractured layout. A glass enclosure opened up the shower, while a tall stainless-steel cabinet serves compact flanking vanities. Designer Sy Iverson chose surfaces based on the couple's talk of apothecary, medical, and hospital elements. "Keying off of those images," he says, "concrete, metal, and glass immediately came to mind."

The antiseptic, easy-clean surfaces are the kind you'd expect in an operating room or a doctor's office. The floor is especially institutional. Iverson laid down a skim coat normally used to level subflooring, applied a brick sealer, and left that as the finished surface.

Color and art soften the hard surfaces and lighten the medical mood. The shower curtain boasts a red cross, and the mosaic-tile shower surfaces are peppered with blue. A pill-theme cartoon, Latin inscriptions, a fake video camera, and X-ray light boxes prove that a roomful of humor helps the medicine go down—in a most delightful way.

ABOVE: **Perky blues lift the spirits of the institutional-look mosaic tile that frames the glass shower enclosure.** OPPOSITE TOP, LEFT: The glass-front medicine chest holds bath supplies as well as apothecary items, including a mortar and pestle that belonged to one of the homeowner's grandmothers. OPPOSITE TOP, RIGHT: **The glass shower enclosure includes a transomlike opening for venting steam.** OPPOSITE BOTTOM, LEFT: **A framed cartoon from *The New Yorker* and X-ray light boxes are quirky cures for the common bath. One box holds an artist's adaptation of a brain scan; the other displays family ultrasound images.** OPPOSITE BOTTOM, RIGHT: Wall-mount faucets and squared-off white sinks add to the doctor's-office feel. **Cherry trim tops the backsplash.**

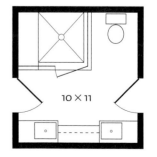

10 × 11

aptly adapted

This classic and comfy bath is full of inspiration for turning an unfinished, awkward attic into a much-used space.

THIS PHOTO: **A comfy window seat disguises unattractive air ducts.**

OPPOSITE: **When floor space and overhead clearance are at a premium, creative design is essential. In this attic bath, shallow cabinetry makes functional storage out of undereaves space.**

An unfinished attic may provide just the space you need for an accommodating bath. But before you call in the contractors, make sure your attic renovation is realistic. The first requirement for this attic makeover was the addition of a staircase. The owners of the 90-year-old Greek Revival took painstaking care to ensure the staircase looked original to the home and provided convenient access from both the upper level and the attic.

The next step in the renovation process was to remove all the loose insulation and replace it with energy-efficient sheets that tuck between the ceiling rafters and wall studs. At its apex, the ceiling in this attic bath is only 8½ feet, so fixtures had to be placed near the high point. A refurbished claw-foot tub is placed away from the wall and a pedestal sink is located just inside the doorway. To accommodate the slope of the ceiling, the owners chose a vanity mirror with a triangular-shape top.

To gain storage but minimize the loss of valuable floor space, the walls beneath the eaves are lined with shallow, affordable stock cabinets (designed as wall-hung models). A custom window seat conceals an unsightly air duct and serves as a favorite perch after a long soak. Variable-width pine boards warm the floor. A soothing color combination of gray-blues and creamy whites completes the scene.

Let There Be Light

Illuminate a bath with a skylight and ceiling fixtures.

ABOVE IT ALL The operable skylight in this bath provides ventilation and supplements the natural light that comes in through the dormer windows.

AUTHENTIC TOUCH The antique pendant fixture, *above*, hangs at the apex of the room. Its aesthetics suited the vintage style of the bath. New wiring made the fixture a safe bet. Its high-lumens output ensures ample light throughout the room.

Thrifty Tips

STORE-BOUGHT GOODS The owners of this bath saved money by using stock cabinets and fixtures from home centers.

SALVAGED STYLE The tub was purchased from an architectural salvage yard and repainted to freshen its look. For the most durable finish, hire a professional.

SHEET SAVVY The curtain panels, window seat cushion, and toss pillows were made from a sheet set. Look for on-sale or clearance items for more savings.

THIS PHOTO: **A paneled ceiling makes the steep slope an architectural detail.** OPPOSITE BOTTOM, LEFT: **To provide privacy, the bath door's glass panels received an application of decorative laminate film.** OPPOSITE BOTTOM, RIGHT: **Brazilian rosewood, purchased on clearance, tops the cabinets.**

from thin air

A designer plays off a bath's angled wall to visually lift its mood and give it some breathing room.

All it took was one look out the windows of this Boston-area condominium, and designer E.J. Krupinsky, a member of the National Kitchen & Bath Association (NKBA), had inspiration for its master bath. With the condo's beautiful harbor views, he knew a nature-inspired design would slip in beautifully indoors.

The renovated space evokes nature through its watery-blue, foggy-gray, and sandy-brown hues; earthy materials; and overall light look. "It's all about water and air," Krupinsky says.

ABOVE: Though it appears to float, the vanity gets support from a slate panel that plays off an angled wall. The door-free blue-tile shower angles into a corner.
OPPOSITE: Open shelves visually lighten the built-in. With cabinets a few inches deeper than standard—and some below the vanity—it's a storage workhorse.

"This room really plays a geometric game. The design is very straightforward and streamlined."

—DESIGNER E.J. KRUPINSKY

The vanity, the first thing visible upon entering the bath, seems to float, setting the stage for the airy atmosphere. On the shower's tiled partial wall, a blue translucent tempered-glass panel rises toward the ceiling, emulating a blue sky.

The room design is about more than a look. It's also about creating a feeling. Large pebble tiles in the shower give bare feet a walking-on-the-beach sensation. "That's about texture and trying to wake somebody up in the morning," Krupinsky says. "It's an ergonomic feeling." And the flow of water from the rain showerhead feels like being in a gentle rainfall.

For Krupinsky, the biggest challenge was making sense of the room's unconventional shape. The entry wall, which is opposite the vanity, angles. It's widest on the end with the shower, then gradually narrows toward the other end, where Krupinsky added a large mahogany built-in that intersperses with the vanity.

Turns out, the not-quite-rectangular shape was a bonus. It gives the room a sense of movement and inspired its clean-lined, linear look. "This room really plays a geometric game," Krupinsky says. "The design is very straightforward and streamlined. There's nothing fussy."

Though streamlined, the room is also full of interest. Grayish slate appears throughout the space, including on the vanity, for continuity. For a visual change-up, Krupinsky shifted the wooden features from light maple on the vanity to rich mahogany for the built-in. "A balance between variety and commonality is really one of the secrets to any room," he says.

Masterful Touches

A stylish, functional bath takes forethought. Consider these tips.

VARIETY SHOW Integrate different materials and textures for interest. "A room gets monotonous if everything is the same," says designer E.J. Krupinsky. In this bath, stone, wood, porcelain, and glass harmonize. Krupinsky mixed two woods—dark mahogany and light maple. "If it were all the same wood, the pieces would just blend in and you wouldn't notice them," he says.

DELIGHTFUL DEPTH When designing your bath, think of it like putting together an outfit: It's not complete until you've added the layers. In this room, mosaic tiles keep walls from falling flat.

SPACE SMARTS Krupinsky considered every corner to eke out storage and function. He had two small slate shelves cut to fit into a corner of the shower, providing landing spots for shampoos and soaps. A petite slate-top bench/footstool angles into another corner. Walls also offer space-efficient storage potential. Go between studs to create a niche in a shower. A recessed medicine cabinet is also a space-saver, and it looks sleeker than a bulky wall-mounted model.

TOP: **Sleek supports on the shower's tempered-glass panel are part of the bath's interesting layers.** TOP RIGHT: **"It's jewelry," designer E.J. Krupinsky says of the mosaic vessel sink.** RIGHT: **A small bench angled into the corner gives the boxy shower a bit more interest.** OPPOSITE: **Mosaic tiles continue from the backsplash onto walls, "blanketing the room like a fabric," Krupinsky says. The mirror reflects the inside of the shower and the glass panel.**

refined beauty

With touches of rich mahogany, this bath suggests English formality. Yet its design is all about boosting the light—and mood.

LEFT: Rounded edges on the wood tub surround lend richness and quality. OPPOSITE: With touches of mahogany, the bath has a traditional look. White walls and wainscoting brighten the room.

For a furnished look, venture beyond bath-aisle offerings. Prop an ornate mirror on a vanity and flank with softly lit sconces instead of hanging a strip of lights above it.

Moderation may have been the mantra for the design of this sophisticated bath. With touches of mahogany, the room is classic and even a bit formal. But architect Jerome Buttrick took care to ensure that the bath didn't take on the persona of a den. "I wanted a masculine, clubby feel common in British design, but without taking it to the extreme," says Buttrick, who limited the mahogany to the vanity and part of the tub surround.

Considering that the primary goal was to brighten the bath, mahogany was a surprising material choice. Prior to the makeover, dark green marble surfaces swallowed the sunlight, the shower was dark and confining, and ornate gold-plated fixtures made the decor ostentatious.

Unifying was Buttrick's first order of business. He covered lower walls with bright white wainscoting and added white-painted moldings above it and at the ceiling. "We wanted to keep the same formal language throughout the house," Buttrick says. Classic limestone floors keep things neutral; with radiant-heat coils installed below, they also ensure that bare feet stay toasty warm. The mahogany gives the neutral shell much-needed contrast, anchoring the room. The result is reminiscent of an English manor—perfect for the 1926 Edwardian-style home.

Buttrick got creative with the shower, exposing it to light without moving the plumbing. He had an opening cut in the wall between the tub and shower, then outfitted it with a tempered-glass panel that matches the new shower door. Sage-green glass mosaic tiles that dress the enclosure reflect light and make the shower inviting from inside. "The green glass has cool, watery overtones," Buttrick says. "People tend to relate to that color in a bathroom because it's soothing and relaxing."

spa
inspiration

2

Baths have become places to relax and rejuvenate.
Jetted tubs and showers with built-in benches and rain showerheads
are common. Underfoot, radiant heating is warming floors—and bare
feet. In general, baths (yes, even small ones) have moved beyond
their utilitarian roles to become indulgences that emulate a spa-like
experience. While the look is often clean and contemporary, spa touches
can be worked into any style of room.

But good looks and pampering amenities aren't the end-all. After all, a
bath still has to perform. When planning your special retreat, make sure
you're not swayed by looks alone. A beautiful tile that's stunning on
shower walls may be too slippery on the floor. A gorgeous, but porous,
countertop may not suit your low-maintenance lifestyle, so look for
more suitable options. As the following baths show, it is possible to
have it both ways—pampering and practical.

clean sweep

With a streamlined design, this tranquil bath goes with the flow.

THIS PHOTO: A niche in the wall provides an extra bit of storage, keeping the vanity clutter-free.
OPPOSITE: With the dark-painted upper walls and ceiling, the bath seems to stretch to infinity.

Looking bigger doesn't need to necessarily mean being bigger.

Matthew Rao, a certified kitchen designer (CKD), realized that when he revamped this 40-square-foot bath in an Atlanta home. Initially he searched for ways to enlarge the space, such as claiming a bedroom closet that backed up to it. But the homeowners decided to keep walls intact, so Rao gave the room the illusion of more square footage.

Streamlining was his approach to achieving spaciousness, as well as spa-inspired style. "It's all about design tricks," Rao says. Clean lines provide an uncluttered look. The vanity is set on legs, and the toilet mounts to the wall for visual breathing room. The same tile climbs all walls before flowing into a deep eggplant-color ceiling. "The ceiling appears to be space instead of another barrier," Rao says.

Another space-enhancer is the shower, enclosed in frameless glass. There's no door and there's no basin curb to step over. "Doors, curbs, steps, moldings—all of those things just create more visual barriers," Rao says. The slightly sloped shower floor directs water to the drain, containing drips.

For Rao, the finished product—a tranquil space full of function—is inspiration that small baths have great potential. "Keep it simple, and a room will feel better and bigger," Rao says. "I've said that for years, but I've never had to prove it in a space quite this small."

ABOVE: A movable mirror layers atop the rectangular mirror, which floats from the wall. "It creates a little more depth and dimension," designer Matthew Rao says. Small lights installed on the wall mirror are another design surprise. LEFT: The faucet provides sleek contrast to the chunky concrete countertop. OPPOSITE TOP, LEFT: Travertine tiles cover all the walls, including in the shower, for a seamless look. The handheld unit allows flexible showering. OPPOSITE TOP, RIGHT: A rain-style showerhead is a pampering luxury. OPPOSITE BOTTOM: Elements that appear to float, including the wall-mounted toilet, contribute to the room's airy look. "It's less visual clutter," Rao says.

Pointers from a Pro

Without changing the location of fixtures or enlarging the room, designer Matthew Rao transformed this pint-size bath into a sleek, soothing retreat. Take inspiration from his ideas.

CONSIDER YOUR ROUTINE Choose surfaces that work with your lifestyle and style preferences. "You have to know what you're getting into," Rao says. For example, a concrete counter is prone to staining and will age over time. "For people who don't want that unpredictability, concrete wouldn't be the right countertop material," Rao says.

STREAMLINE The adage "Less is more" is especially true in a small space. Rao ran tile seven feet up the walls and steered clear of moldings to minimize visual starts and stops.

WEIGH THE PROS AND CONS "There are consequences to any decision," Rao says. In this bath, he knew a curbless, doorless shower wasn't foolproof. "We traded a few instances where you might get a little spillage outside the shower for having a room that looks, feels, and is so much cleaner and freer visually," he says.

guest privileges

A guest bath once plagued by plumbing problems is now functioning beautifully and flush with perks.

RIGHT: **A glass door showcases new tile, while a half-wall hides the toilet. The handheld showerhead has a holder that adjusts to guests of varying heights.**
OPPOSITE: **Warm colors, fresh flowers, and stacks of soft white towels make a welcoming guest bath.**

The dream of a pampering guest bath seemed far from the reality that Jeanne and Harold Egler faced at their home in Redmond, Washington. The existing guest bath had a leaky shower, moldy walls (due to a lack of ventilation), a drafty disposition (due to a lack of insulation), and a cranky commode. "When the toilet overflowed during a party, we decided it was time for a change," Jeanne says. The couple hired Sheila Tilander, a certified kitchen and bath designer (CKD/CBD) and member of the National Kitchen & Bath Association (NKBA), to redesign the 1970s main-level bath. "We wanted to give it a generally updated look, fix the water leaks, and provide better ventilation," Tilander says.

Structural realities prevented the bath from being enlarged, so Tilander simply gutted the space and started from scratch. New plumbing and ventilation systems stopped the leaks and solved the mold problem. "Before, I'd actually have to wipe the walls down with bleach after long showers to avoid mold buildup," Jeanne says. "Now it's something I don't have to worry about." Insulating the wall between the shower and the adjacent garage alleviated the chronic chilliness.

Without changing the footprint of the small bath, Tilander strove to make the 5×10-foot space look bigger than its dimensions suggest. For example, she traded the existing shower door—a 1970s-look model with a metal frame and obscured glass—for a frameless, clear-glass version that allows an unobstructed view of stylish new tile inside. "The frameless shower door makes it look bigger and not as closed in," Tilander says.

The shower's 12-inch-square beige tiles are part of a warm, light palette that further expands the room visually and creates a sense of calmness. Dazzling amber-glass mosaic tiles complement the larger tiles throughout the room, including on the floor in front of the vanity, where Tilander designed a tile inset that imitates an area rug. "We love the little glass mosaic tiles and the big tiles on the shower wall," Jeanne says. "I was looking for a large tile so there wouldn't be a lot of grout to clean."

The new vanity is a console-style cherrywood unit with storage above and below. A glass shelf holds extra towels, while trumpet-shape sconces flank an oval mirror that fronts a medicine cabinet. "It's nice to have a medicine cabinet that doesn't look like a medicine cabinet," Jeanne says. A half-wall separates the vanity from the toilet niche, where a cherry cabinet with a frosted-glass door provides more storage.

The clever storage, sense of openness, and updated look have turned a host's worst nightmare into a guest's dream.

ABOVE: **Glass tiles anchor the corners of an "area rug" created with different shapes of tiles.**
OPPOSITE: **The curves of the sink complement an oval mirror that conceals a medicine cabinet.**

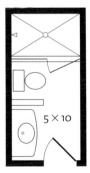

5 × 10

Eliminating a doorway allowed the tub and shower to share a wall in this bath, saving space in tight quarters.

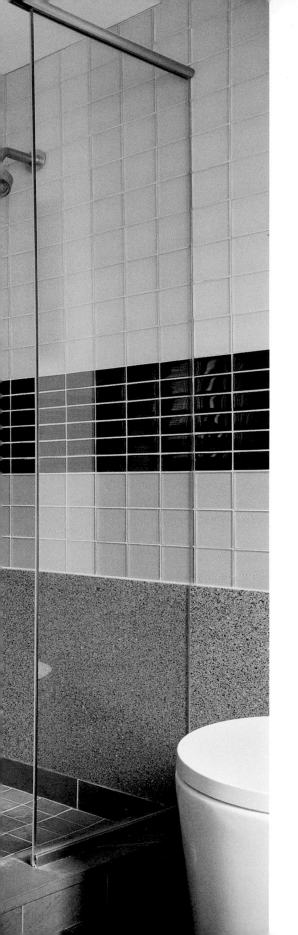

seasoned serenity

New Age style and age-old space coexist peacefully in a modern-look master bath with ties to tradition.

Call it a December-May redo. The master bath in the penthouse of a 19th-century Boston townhome was in the winter of its life and definitely showing its age. The homeowner wanted to invigorate her bath with the spring freshness of a brand-new spa.

Trouble is, all the modern amenities she wanted—a deep soaking tub for two, a glass-enclosed shower, and a long vanity—simply would not fit into a 9×9-foot room where two doorways broke up the walls and historic-district rules dictated the window's size.

A design team led by E.J. Krupinsky, a member of the National Kitchen & Bath Association (NKBA), turned less into more by letting the bath's box shape inspire a functional new layout. After Krupinsky eliminated one of the doors—creating a wall for the tub and shower to share—he faced the challenge of the window. "That was the only place left for the vanity," Krupinsky says. "And that was a problem because the neighbors can look right in, and the glare made it hard to apply makeup."

To provide privacy for the homeowner and filter the harsh sunlight, Krupinsky had all but one of the divided-light window's 12 panes covered with translucent film. Then he mounted a pivoting mirror on a pole in front of the window, framing the mirror to complement the style of the window. When the vanity mirror is turned to one side, the clear pane near the center of the window is exposed, offering a peek outdoors. And the window can still be opened to

provide a wider view, bring in fresh air, and offer access to the building's fire escape.

The size of the room prohibited a separate area for the toilet, so the design team took an artistic approach and hid the fixture in plain sight. An expanse of gray-green quartz on the wall between the shower and vanity serves as the backdrop for a low-profile, hatbox-style model. The treatment elevates the toilet into an avant-garde sculpture, a solution that particularly pleased the homeowner, who is a painter.

Though the bath is mostly contemporary in style, historical references to the surrounding Beacon Hill neighborhood abound in the architectural detailing, colors, and materials. The mirror pole draws inspiration from the black cast-iron balconies that the window overlooks, the brushed-nickel sink faucet recalls the old-fashioned pipe fountains found in the area, and the gray slate around the tub and shower matches that on the building's front steps. Colorful glass tile conveys the beauty of stained-glass windows, while birch cabinetry and cherry flooring incorporate the traditional richness of wood.

The fresh look for the formerly tired bath has created a new feeling of serenity in the space, something the owner appreciates in December, May, and every other month of the year.

ABOVE: The tub spout is set into a slate shelf inspired by the home's front steps. BELOW LEFT: The vanity features a pivoting mirror and light fixtures that mimic candles. BELOW RIGHT: Turning the mirror exposes a lone clear pane in the window. The other panes are covered in film to provide privacy and cut glare. OPPOSITE: Contemporary shapes and surfaces in the vanity area bring a modern spa feel to the 19th-century space.

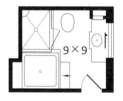

practical magic

A floating vanity, reflective surfaces, and a light color scheme make this master bath live large.

They may be veteran remodelers, but John Friswell and Adriana Palomares aren't magicians. The master bath in their Vancouver rambler, though, suggests quite the contrary. The husband-and-wife team, who own a renovation firm, injected their creativity— and eye-catching illusions—into their master bath retreat.

Before the remodel, one small, outdated bath serviced the home's three bedrooms. Because John and Adriana weren't using all three rooms, they converted one into a master bath connected to the master bedroom. The new space comfortably accommodates the couple's desired amenities—a large walk-in shower, ample storage, separate sinks, and a toilet compartment—with room to spare.

Simple yet elegant surface materials, including pale yellow walls and large, earthy travertine tiles, instantly open the room, making it appear larger. And they allow prominent features, especially the vanity, to stand out. Positioned against

OPPOSITE: The vanity provides ample storage, keeping the top clutter-free. Floating shelves keep towels and other necessities close at hand.

a long wall, dark-stained maple floating cabinets form the vanity base, topped by white vessel sinks to emphasize the clean lines. Side cabinets flank the vanity, providing extra storage and visual balance.

The entire vanity wall is eye-catching. Floating shelves corral bath essentials, while two large, custom-framed mirrors— one above each sink—reflect light around the room. And overhead, a custom bulkhead with amber-glass light fixtures radiates warmth. "We wanted to make the vanity a focal point," Adriana says.

Strategically positioned between the vanity and the shower, a large window floods the space with natural light, which heightens the sense of spaciousness as it reflects off the shower's seamless glass door. The walk-in shower features spa-inspired luxuries, such as a heated floor, a corner bench made of travertine, and dual showerheads, perfect for pampering. A travertine tile mosaic mingles with light-reflective white ceramic tile for a look that's timeless yet low-maintenance. Next to the shower, decorative sconces in the toilet compartment brighten the shower, thanks to two glass panels that flank the plumbing column.

The illusion of spaciousness isn't the only design trick the couple used in this bath. Though the materials and fixtures look high-end, they're actually stylish middle-of-the-line fixtures Adriana found scouting out suppliers on the Internet.

"It's important to look at trends and then shop around to get the look you want for less," John says.

In a space defined by design illusions, one thing isn't a trick: John and Adriana love the timeless character of their new en suite retreat. "It's contemporary and neutral," John says. "This isn't going to fall out of style soon."

ABOVE LEFT: The simple, curved lines of the vessel sinks and faucets embody the room's classic contemporary design. ABOVE: This luxurious showerhead offers a relaxing, rainlike spray. OPPOSITE: A simple glass door showcases the compact shower's features, including elegant tilework, a travertine bench, and fixed and handheld showerheads.

PLAN PRIORITIES
The homeowners opted for a large walk-in shower in place of a tub to maximize their small space.

tranquil translation

A Japanese-style master bath that's just 5x9 feet provides a soothing respite from the 9-to-5 grind.

RIGHT: A pocket door saves space and heightens the Asian appeal with its shoji-screen design.
OPPOSITE: A water-filled Japanese garden outside inspired the design of this bath. Wooden steps lead to a soaking tub. A big window admits soothing sights and sounds.

ABOVE: Though the vanity doors feature a shoji-screen pattern, designer Michael Ranson filled the recessed portions with copper instead of paper to match the sink. ABOVE RIGHT: The hammered-copper sink boasts natural color variations and a fountainlike faucet. OPPOSITE LEFT: Rugged-edge myrtle wood steps, cantilevered along the bamboo tub apron, seem to float above stones. OPPOSITE RIGHT: The tub filler mimics the look and sound of trickling water in the garden outside.

A trickle of water has launched

many a bath remodel. In this case, though, it didn't come from an aggravating leak, but from a soothing stream. Interior designer Michael Ranson drew on the water features of a Japanese garden just outside as inspiration for a peaceful, spa-inspired master bath in Coronado, California.

The 5×9-foot space was not always soothing. "It was the typical bathroom—a standard tub with a small window, a toilet, and a sink," Ranson says. The homeowners, enamored of Japanese culture, wanted the bathroom to complement the fusion style in the rest of their home.

To do that, Ranson surrounded a Japanese-style soaking tub with an earthy and serene interior landscape. The tub—called a furo in Japan—is nearly 3 feet deep. Split bamboo covers the tall apron front; cantilevered myrtle wood steps that "float" over a bed of pebbles provide access. "When I design I am thinking in terms of layers and textures," Ranson says. "The flooring is dark slate tile to ground the space, and

the bed of pebbles reinforces the sensation of crossing over into the garden." The tub's honed black granite decking adds yet another layer.

To accommodate the large tub, Ranson reconfigured the layout, moving the toilet and sink and eliminating a door to the bedroom. The old passageway now holds a freestanding-look custom vanity. "Because it doesn't touch the surrounding walls and it has furniture-style feet, it creates the illusion of space," Ranson says. He topped the vanity with the same granite used for the tub deck and paired it with a hammered-copper sink. "The granite has brown in it that plays well off the copper sink and ties the look together," he says.

To free space and add more Asian style, Ranson replaced the traditional swinging entry door with a pocket unit reminiscent of a shoji screen. He also turned a bit of closet space from the adjacent bedroom into built-in shelving.

The tranquillity of the Japanese garden just outside is an integral part of the new look. A large window over the tub provides pleasing garden views and opens to filter in the soothing sounds of moving water. A shoji screen–style window treatment that matches the door provides privacy when desired.

Keeping with the earthy, natural theme, Ranson rounded out the room by covering the walls in grass cloth and installing bronze-finish faucets and hardware. "This was all about a pleasing balance between the materials," he says, "taking into consideration color and texture and creating a beautiful retreat."

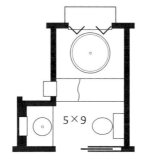

5 × 9

a little massaging

Tension-relieving tweaks and sensuous surfaces turn a master bath into an inviting retreat.

Even a modest-size bath can enjoy a little luxury. After seven years of sharing an awkward, outdated space, Melinda and Pat Andrew were ready for some pampering. "We wanted to make it warm and inviting," Melinda says of the 9×9-foot master bath in her Lake Oswego, Oregon, home.

The couple called on Keri Davis, a certified kitchen designer (CKD) and member of the National Kitchen & Bath Association (NKBA). Davis tweaked the limited layout and upgraded the look, introducing elegant finishes and a few unexpected touches.

A consistent, serene palette of natural materials is essential to a luxurious look, Davis says. In this case, Melinda was drawn to a soft yellow limestone for the shower walls and vanity counter. The wall paint and subway tiles carry complementing colors throughout the room.

Underfoot, a pebbled tile floor blends with the scheme but stands out for its unusual texture. "It's a really interesting and unique element," Melinda says. "It

THIS PHOTO: **A limestone shower, dark-wood double vanity, and pebbled tile floor—a foot massage in every step—detail this master bath.**
OPPOSITE: **Limestone that lines the shower also tops the vanity, which is backed by crisp subway tiles on the wainscoting.**

massages the feet and provides a very spa-like feel."

Against the pale backdrop, dark wood elements enrich the atmosphere. Trading in a typical boxy vanity for a custom-made open-bottom one instantly made the bath look bigger. "I appreciate the simplicity of it," Melinda says. "I didn't want all the drawers and cabinets you usually see. I love seeing the subway tile underneath and a little bit of the plumbing."

The vanity area lives large now, thanks to a second sink and a pair of recessed medicine cabinets. "Going from one sink to two is really what makes a small bath work for two people," Melinda says. "The medicine cabinet feature was brilliant. For storage of essentials, it's much better than having to bend down and fish through drawers."

For more storage, part of a hall closet was folded into the bath. Another floor-plan fix subtracted space from the toilet area and added it to the shower. The divider between the two changed from a full wall to a half-wall topped with glass, further opening the room and allowing a freer flow of light.

To augment an existing skylight, Davis placed sconces and recessed fixtures on dimmers. Melinda found the final touch: a chandelier that punctuates the room. "It's perfection— something special in a simple space," Melinda says.

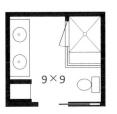

9 × 9

ABOVE LEFT: The frameless clear-glass shower enclosure adds an upscale European feel. The glass helps the space seem larger. ABOVE: The couple kept things simple inside the shower, forgoing fancy showerheads but including a built-in bench. OPPOSITE: Two sinks instead of one are a luxury the homeowners enjoy every day. A linen closet and recessed medicine chests are alternatives to undersink storage. Prettier items are displayed on the vanity's lower shelf.

dramatic flair

An artful niche and golden tiles make the tub area of this bath the center of attention.

ABOVE: **The tub's backlit niche, matted in white tiles, mimics the look of framed artwork.** OPPOSITE: **Built-in wall shelves and open storage in a cherry vanity keep towels, soaps, and lotions in easy reach—and the room clean of clutter.**

Part of a former servants' quarters, this small bath in a 1928 home was stripped to the studs and rebuilt to span a century of style—and provide modern comfort. A window was the room's only distinguishing feature, leaving interior designer Leslie Harris free to create an entirely new personality that merges the old with the new. She used stunning tiles, traditional wood, and metallic accents to fast-forward this bath nearly 100 years.

A vanity, mirror, and built-in wall shelves, all of cherry, are traditional furniture-like pieces. Metallic finishes on the sink, faucets, and fittings allude to the elegance and excess of the roaring '20s, when the home was built. Golden crackle-finish field tiles extend floor to ceiling in the tub surround and add a colorful contemporary feel.

Harris designed a backlit niche above the tub as a dramatic focal point. Like matted artwork, it catches the eye of anyone entering the room and casts enhancing, warm light onto the surrounding tiles. The artful feature also makes relaxing in the tub for a long soak even more of a pleasure.

sea change

Once a total washout, this bathroom now makes a splash with its pampering shower and ocean-inspired detailing.

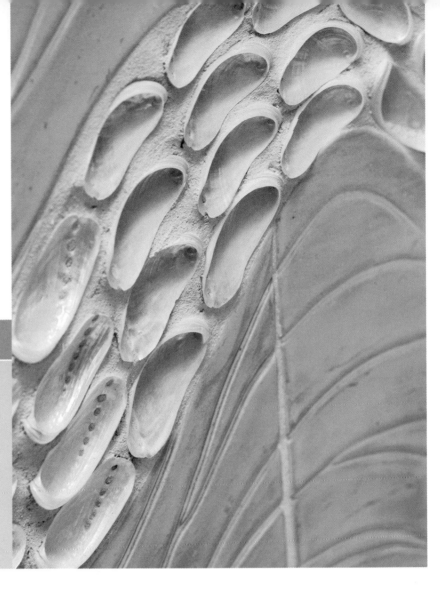

RIGHT: **Abalone shells create a rolling wave of textural interest.**
OPPOSITE: **Because it doesn't reach the floor, the floating vanity enhances a sense of space. It also provides plenty of storage in drawers designed for grooming essentials and linens.**

Custom Approach

PERSONAL TOUCHES Handcrafted items, such as tile, were incorporated to reflect the homeowners' love of the ocean.

LIGHT LOOK The floating vanity gives the room an upscale look.

SAVE AND SPLURGE The homeowners spent more on items that need to stand the test of time, such as fixtures and the pampering shower system, and less on trendy accessories, such as the mirror.

Free-form waves of tile undulate across the walls of Jolee Pink's bath. The tiles—created by Jolee, who has a ceramic studio in the garage of her Encinitas, California, home—mimic the nearby ocean scene and established the mood for this hall bathroom redo.

"I was inspired by walks on the beach viewing the ocean," Jolee says about the tiles, which took two months to produce. "Each tile is handmade and seemed to take forever to make." Jolee drew a large template on multiple pieces of butcher-block paper, then transferred the shapes and lines to raw clay. "This ensured that each column of tile, and the sculpted lines within, would flow into the next," she says. "Then I experimented with different glaze combinations before settling on two different colors that, when layered, created the perfect aqua hue."

Jolee especially enjoys the handmade, tactile nature of the tile and how its color depth contrasts with the abalone shells handset into the tile. "In a soothing way, it encircles the room and creates the illusion of water," she says.

All that is quite a change for a space Jolee and her husband, Larry, once called the "linoleum room" because of its outdated yellow flooring with matching harvest gold prefab tub-and-shower combo. Chipped countertops topped generic white cabinets.

From the get-go, the couple agreed that only a complete renovation would do. "At just 53 square feet, the bathroom was just a small, overstuffed rectangle with nothing going for it designwise," Jolee says. "So we gutted the space and started over."

As the owner of an eco-art design firm, Jolee devised a design incorporating smart planning and

features that foster the illusion of space. For example, clear glass doors that enclose the spa-like shower maintain unimpeded sight lines to the shower, lined in a mosaic of eco-friendly vitrified glass tiles—a budget splurge—that sparkle like gems on the walls above serene aqua ceramic flooring.

Contributing to the serenity is the floating vanity in African mahogany. Designed by Jolee, it not only introduces a marine element but also echoes the rich color and beautiful grain of flooring throughout the house. Accent lights beneath the cabinet enhance the design and eliminate shadows on the cream-color travertine flooring.

Flooding the space with bright coastal sunshine, the skylight in the center of the room keeps the space functional by augmenting a lone window in the shower area. Light bounces off walls meticulously painted with a water-, mold-, and mildew-resistant finish called Shimmerstone. Tinted to match the floor, the luminous paint adds subtle depth while reflecting light and bringing out the pearl-like sheen of abalone shells embedded in the tile border.

Because the couple's budget was limited, they did much of the work themselves. Jolee served as designer, general contractor, tile-maker, and finisher. Larry gutted the space and installed the plumbing fixtures, faucets, fan, and lighting. Smart shopping and balancing investment and discount buys kept them on budget.

What once gave Jolee nightmares now beckons all who enter to dream in Neptune-inspired Technicolor. "We took a bland, nothing room and transformed it into a piece of art," Jolee says.

ABOVE RIGHT: **Fresh flowers in a glass wall pocket instill another natural element.** RIGHT: **Instead of multiple exposed shower elements that visually clutter, the showerhead, thermostatic controls, body jets, and hand-held spray are housed in a single shower panel.** OPPOSITE: **Windows in the oversize shower bring natural light into the room.**

straight away

With clean lines and neutral colors, a sense of calm prevails in this refreshingly simple guest bath.

Simplicity was the key to creating a comfortable, stylish guest bath out of a narrow connecting room in a historical Philadelphia townhouse. Architect Christopher Beardsley lined up the vanity, tub and shower combination, and toilet along one wall, leaving the opposite wall—painted a fresh periwinkle—free for towel bars and movement from one end of the bath to the other.

"We tried to focus not just on the individual fixtures, but on what was happening in between," Beardsley says. The vanity countertop connects to a half-wall at one end of the tub, tying the two elements together. The opposite end of the tub features a similar half-wall, but with a chimneylike extension in the middle to accommodate a showerhead. Glass panels help contain shower spray and make the narrow space feel less confining.

The built-in vanity also helps the 5×12-foot bath feel larger, Beardsley says. "It's supposed to float simply, and not be like a big, clunky cabinet."

To complement the simple design, Beardsley chose a limited palette of colors and surfaces—gray limestone for the countertop, maple for the cabinet, and carrara marble tiles for the walls and floor. "You can't put too many materials in a small room, or it would fracture," Beardsley says.

Though the look of the bath is clearly contemporary, Beardsley did retain some period architectural elements in the space, such as the two 100-year-old doors and the traditional molding around them. The integration of styles proves that a narrow space need not be subject to a narrow-minded approach.

OPPOSITE: **Architect Christopher Beardsley used the same marble tiles on the backsplash, tub and shower walls, and floor to lend color consistency and simplify this small guest bath.**

5 × 12

A simple, straight-line arrangement of fixtures follows the room shape instead of fighting it, leaving a clear passage between the two doors. The tub-shower unit saves space and offers bathing options, yet it has the feel of a stand-alone walk-in. The door by the vanity opens out, allowing more room to move inside the bath.

RIGHT: The vanity exemplifies the uncluttered design, with an above-counter sink and minimalist faucet atop a simple limestone slab and maple cabinet. OPPOSITE: Having all the fixtures on one wall fosters spaciousness in the narrow bath, as does glass around the combination tub and shower.

colorful history

Spa-style indulgences refresh a 1930s bath while still respecting its vintage spirit.

THIS PHOTO: A console-style sink with a marble top saves space while creating spa style.

OPPOSITE: The wall tile adds modern flair while drawing on the colors of vintage stained glass.

A city boy who would never live in the suburbs, Frank Simokaitis settled in a 75-year-old Tudor Revival near downtown St. Louis. Frank and his wife, Dee, loved the home's architecture and spacious rooms but not its outdated master bath. "It wasn't the style that we liked," Frank says. "It was built in the '30s and reflected that." Dated tile, old plumbing fixtures, and a cramped floor plan all needed upgrading. "We were looking for more of the spa experience," he says.

The couple wanted a large shower, a separate tub for bathing their twins, and plenty of room to get ready in the morning. They asked designer Stacy Hillman to include it all without enlarging the approximately 70-square-foot bath. To create more floor space within the existing footprint, she removed a linen closet, rotated the toilet, fitted the entry for a pocket door, and replaced a radiator with an under-the-floor heating system that extends partway up the exterior wall.

Once Hillman settled on the best arrangement for the main amenities—a built-in whirlpool tub, a spacious shower with two heads and a bench, and a console-style sink—she used visual tricks to increase the sense of space. For example, she extended the stone flooring up the wall, using it as a baseboard to make the floor seem wider and deeper. She used a high tile wainscoting, extending it to the windowsill to elongate the walls and play up the high ceilings. The sink console, an open frame that reveals the floor, provides a roomier look than a conventional cabinet.

Hillman also made use of mirrors. "The thing that really makes a big difference in this bathroom is using that plate glass mirror on one wall," Frank says. "It opens up the space and makes you feel that the bathroom is so much larger." The frameless design enhances the effect.

Vintage-look faucets and hardware tie the bath to the home's architectural era, as does an original stained-glass window. But the colors of the stained glass translate into more contemporary tile designs, including a glass mosaic pattern that covers shower walls and trims the tub and wainscoting. "Everything in the bathroom seems to fit together like it was meant to be," Frank says.

ABOVE LEFT: **The homeowners wanted a spacious tub for their young children. A handheld showerhead is handy for washing hair.** ABOVE: **Mosaic tiles help the generous shower seem even larger. A steam option provides the spa-like luxury the couple desired.** OPPOSITE: **Designer Stacy Hillman's challenge was to make the bath feel bigger without changing the room's footprint. One way she did this was by extending the tile wainscoting up to the windowsill, thereby increasing the perceived height of the walls.**

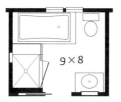

9 × 8

sheer luxury

A designer's light touch ensures that this master bath is easy on the eyes and good for the mind.

THIS PHOTO: **Sleek, straight-line design and a light, limited color palette simplify this bath.**
OPPOSITE: **Accessories echo the natural mix of glass, stone, and wood.**

Different types of glass provide light and openness, obscuring views where desired and showcasing luxurious materials.

Designer Mick De Giulio, famed for his kitchens, is adept at baths, too. "The principles of design are the same, even though the functionalities are different," he says.

De Giulio used those principles to transform the modest-size master bath of this Chicago-area home. The 1950s space had been remodeled in the 1980s—and looked it. The owners' willingness to sacrifice a whirlpool tub created new possibilities. "That opened us up to doing a larger, more luxurious shower, and opened the door to a clean, wide-open design," De Giulio says.

The shower's glass block window and glass double doors complement light-color limestone walls and floor. "You walk in and the shower is just a breath of fresh air," De Giulio says.

In keeping with the sleek, rectilinear design, he chose square sinks for the vanity and mounted a frameless three-way mirror above it. The mirror, lit from above and below, appears to float on the wall. Open shelves and a storage cabinet with sanded-glass doors convey the same weightless feeling. "The sanded glass gives that transparency so you see the color and form coming through," De Giulio says.

A narrow, neutral color palette and a short list of exquisite materials further opened the space and freed it from a weighty past. "We started with something very dated, and ended with something that's classic," De Giulio says.

10 × 10

TOP LEFT AND RIGHT: **Sanded-glass doors on a tall cabinet near the shower obscure everyday bath supplies, while open niches above and elsewhere show off art and items that have more visual appeal.** ABOVE: **Designer Mick De Giulio chose faucets with high-arc spouts to throw a curve into the rectilinear design. The metal finish also stands out against low-sheen countertops of flamed-and-brushed granite.** OPPOSITE: **The shower's glass double doors—aligned with the glass block window—swing both ways for better ventilation, safety, and ease of use. The French-limestone interior includes a built-in bench.**

THIS PHOTO: **A rain showerhead is a luxurious touch in the small shower. The space-saving sliding door has frosted glass to provide privacy.**
OPPOSITE: **Vertical tiles visually stretch the room.**

smooth moves

Heated flooring, taller-than-usual fixtures, and a few little luxuries prove that an ultra-sleek space can be filled with comfort.

The word "comfort" conjures images of softness—cushy pillows, cozy throws, and sink-into-it sofas and chairs. In a bathroom, however, hard surfaces are the norm, so comfort is wrapped in a slightly different package.

In this sleek-looking Manhattan bath, the comforting features are subtle, even hidden. Radiant heat installed under the tile warms the floor—and bare feet. "It's a luxury I can't imagine being without," says homeowner Jon Monahan. The vanity is set a bit higher than is standard to accommodate Jon's height. And Jon cleverly used a kitchen faucet to gain even more height. "I don't need to bend over too much to brush my teeth—not sure why no one else has thought of it," he says.

Physical comfort aside, the remodeled space also accommodates creature comforts. A wall-mounted flat-screen TV allows Jon to catch the morning news while he's getting ready for work. The shower stall may be narrow, but its rain showerhead still pampers. And the deep tub provides an additional place to relax. Comfort, indeed.

Size things up
Want a more user-friendly bath? These ideas do the trick.

RISE TO THE OCCASION When choosing a vanity, pick a taller model to avoid stooping. A kitchen base cabinet, which is taller, can work as a vanity, too. And as homeowner Jon Monahan can attest, a kitchen faucet is a slick way to eke out more height. Toilets are also getting taller; look for ones marked as "comfort height."

CLEAR THE WAY In a small shower, a wall niche will keep soaps and bottles out of the way, ultimately giving you more room to move. It's also a cleaner look than a caddy dangling from the shower head.

LEFT: A niche—tall and narrow to echo the tile—provides a landing spot for shampoo and soap. ABOVE: A kitchen faucet adds an extra bit of height. With any faucet, make sure the sink is deep enough to accommodate the spray. OPPOSITE: The tall, slim mirror plays off the vertical tiles on the floor and shower wall and offers contrast to the mosaic tiles.

powder room finesse

3

A powder room should be a treat for the eyes. Small in size, it's the perfect space to play around in. Imagine glass tiles shimmering on walls or leather squares providing high-style coziness. Perhaps it's creative touches—a sink that folds into the wall or a ceiling-mounted satin curtain that hides less-sightly features—that impress. The powder rooms that follow are filled with such inspiration.

Take a look around your powder room to see where it could use a little boost. Adding drama can be as simple as painting walls or hanging a thick-framed mirror. But why stop there? These little gems are manageable remodeling projects. The sink wall is usually the focal point, so put the emphasis there. A new vanity, sink, countertop, and faucet can work wonders. With a tile backsplash or perhaps a textural wall covering, it may seem like you have a new room. In fact, a well-conceived powder room can set the tone for an entire home. Go ahead and take yours beyond basic-box status.

steps to style

It may be just 35 inches wide, but this sophisticated space still packs a visual punch.

As designer Jeni Wright worked her renovation magic on a kitchen in a 1913 home, she frequently went in and out of the back entryway. Every time she passed the opening where a short staircase used to be, she couldn't help but envision a more practical use of the little, dark space.

Today, a polished powder room nestles in the cozy space—just 15 square feet—that once was a staircase. Compact and convenient, the new bathroom blends with the decor of the Des Moines home like it was part of the original blueprint.

Though enamored with the space, Wright knew it had design challenges. For instance, the room is only 35 inches wide. To work with such a narrow dimension, Wright chose a round vanity, just under 21 inches wide, that fits snugly into a corner. Its curved shape eliminates the need to dodge sharp edges, and its corner design utilizes space usually wasted in a bath.

To extend the line of vision, Wright hung a tall, narrow mirror above the vanity and flanked it with wall sconces at face level.

"Using that corner for the vanity and the mirror was the only solution that allowed the door to completely open," Wright says. "But it's good to know that not everything has to be placed on a flat wall."

Neutral colors underscore the sense of space and depth in a room, so Wright selected a nature-inspired

taupe-and-white wallpaper. She chose a tumbled slate floor with a small mosaic design in shades of taupe, brown, gray, and cream. This durable covering extends into the back entryway.

"This was another way to keep the room from feeling so small," Wright says. "By continuing the flooring out into the entryway, the whole space feels a little larger and connected to another area."

White baseboards echo a design touch that appears throughout the Craftsman-style house. To hide ductwork, Wright built a ledge on the wall adjacent to the toilet and had it painted white to match the baseboards. It creates the perfect spot for decorative accessories.

"It's really handy for guests—and the family—to have a powder room on the first floor," Wright says.

LEFT: Simple accessories, such as birch branches, enhance the room's back-to-nature design theme. Hefty white-painted baseboards add a crisp touch. ABOVE: Designer Jeni Wright selected a faucet with a satin-nickel finish and white ceramic levers. Inspired by early-20th-century design, it perfectly complements the home's style. OPPOSITE: The vanity's small drawer and low shelf provide storage for guest towels and toiletries. A taupe glaze covers the cast-iron sink, carrying out the room's monochromatic decor.

winning metals

Wood, metal, and stone bolster a powder room that's dramatic yet not too serious.

No two powder rooms are the same for designer Lori Carroll, a member of the National Kitchen & Bath Association (NKBA). "When I do powder rooms, I want to make each one look different," she says.

The remodeled powder room in Lori's 1990 Tucson home shows her penchant for creating distinctive-looking spaces. She mixed heavy materials in a lighthearted way. "It's always about the materials," Lori says. "I love mixing materials in unusual ways."

An oak vanity with a metal top and vessel sink is the focal point of the room, enclosed by side walls that are tiled in a playful checkerboard pattern and edged with metal moldings. The back wall, covered in metallic-finish cork wallpaper, holds a large mirror framed in more metal.

"I walk by the powder room every day, and it's fun to look at," Lori says.

ABOVE RIGHT: Stamped-concrete floor tiles ground the space. RIGHT: The bronze-finish sink rests on a metal-topped oak vanity. FAR RIGHT: Portal-look sidelights pop out playfully from tiles set in a checkerboard pattern.

6 × 8

hall pass

An ingenious design (check out the sink!) liberates a linen closet into a much-used bath.

Wanting an extra bath but not the expense of an addition, Christy and Steve McAvoy eyed a hall linen closet that backed up to a utility closet in the kitchen of their Ventura, California, home. Knowing it would take ingenuity, they turned to Christy's brother, John Tucker, a designer, builder, and artist with a unique way of looking at things.

"The space is only 38 inches by 57 inches," Tucker says of the challenging proposal. "I first figured out that although a toilet could be installed, there wouldn't be any room for a sink." The solution? A sink that recedes into the wall—a sink in a drawer. A sewer pipe and standard sink plumbing were run into the back of an adjacent kitchen cabinet; flexible spa hose was attached to allow the drawer to pull out. "That part was tricky because the hose wants to pull the drawer back in," Tucker says. "There has to be a delicate balance between the shape and length of the hose and the balance of the drawer."

The powder room cost about $5,000. For Christy and Steve, it beat building an addition. "It's making use of what you have in a creative way," Christy says.

ABOVE LEFT: The powder room's space-saving features include vertical display niches retrofitted between wall studs and a mahogany bifold door that provides clearance when opening and closing from inside. FAR LEFT AND LEFT: The so-called "sink-in-a-drawer" features a small stainless-steel bowl set in a mosaic of gray glass tiles. The drawer balance keeps the sink from sliding in when in use. Faucet and handles are mounted on the wall above.

beauty from the basin

An angled vanity puts a new slant on a boxy space, drawing attention to the artful vessel sink.

A sand-cast white-bronze basin, crafted by a San Francisco artist, provided the inspiration for this minimalist powder room. "I wanted to do something unusual, something that was distinctive," homeowner Diane Garrett says. To achieve the sleek look they envisioned, Diane and her husband, Todd, set the basin atop an angled blue-gray French limestone countertop.

To continue transforming the 5×6-foot small and windowless room into a functional and sophisticated space, the Garretts added a custom-made vanity that has a small, subtle drawer Diane stocks with convenience items for guests.

Traditional grass cloth adds a warm texture to the walls while the maple mirror and Japanese-style contemporary light fixtures contribute to the serenity. The platinum-finish wall-mount faucet mimics the sink's texture and contemporary form while saving valuable counter space.

LEFT: The small room's mix of materials, shapes, and textures achieves the perfect balance of uncluttered serenity and luxury. ABOVE: The sleek, custom-designed cabinet floats above the white wood floor. The small drawer is nearly imperceptible when closed. OPPOSITE: The bronze basin, angled limestone countertop, and grass-cloth wallcovering blend function with Asian-style serenity.

eco-rich elegance

Easy on the eyes, this warm and inviting powder room was also easy on the environment.

It's the burgundy of glass mosaic tiles that catches the eye, but designer Laura Birns made sure that green is just as important in this California powder room. Birns used eco-friendly yet elegant materials throughout.

Wenge and eucalyptus wood for the custom vanity cabinetry came from managed forests and was stained with products low in volatile organic compounds (VOCs). The concrete countertop is embedded with recycled glass, the lighting is low-voltage, and the paints are low in VOCs. The flooring is recycled wood.

Though the room's impact on the planet is low, its impact on the home is high: The powder room is just inside the front entry, greeting guests with a dynamic mix of colors, shapes, and patterns. "The space packs a subtle punch as the individual materials and pieces are observed," Birns says. "However, the overall look is the first impression."

ABOVE LEFT: **Burgundy tile in a bamboo pattern sets a colorfully contemporary tone in this powder room. Eco-friendly materials show off the glamorous side of green.** LEFT: **A solid granite basin sits on a concrete countertop that incorporates flecks of recycled glass.**

5 × 10

petite sparkle

Reflective surfaces and artistic details help this space beautifully stand out.

With so many elegant touches, it's difficult to image that this jewel of a powder room was formerly a humble hall closet in a Minneapolis home. "The homeowners sought a memorable, glamorous powder room while staying within the context of the 1920s-built home," interior designer Carol Belz says. "You actually have a 'wow' sensation by just walking into such a small space and seeing that every square inch is so thoughtfully produced."

Overlapping mirrors and crystal detailing provide sparkle. But the most impressive feature is the vanity. With a painted design on its front, the vanity is a true work of art.

The long, shallow vanity is also graced with a marble top, an oval sink, a showy wall-mount faucet, and a gracefully curved front. It's open below to save space, adding dressing-table elegance. "The vanity extends the length of the room, helping the space feel bigger," architect Jean Rehkamp Larson says.

> **"You actually have a 'wow' sensation ... every square inch is so thoughtfully produced."**
>
> —DESIGNER CAROL BELZ

ABOVE LEFT: **A framed mirror overlaps a wall-length version, making the small powder room seem larger. The vanity front was custom-painted to resemble an antique lacquered tray.** LEFT: **Crystal faucet handles and a hammered-nickel sink are among the room's luxurious touches.**

3½ × 5

warming trend

Leather-clad walls give this space high-style comfort.

Part of a home designed specifically for entertaining, this powder room sees a lot of guest traffic—thanks not only to its convenient location, but also to its artistic look. Leather wall tiles stretch a canvas for a two-piece marble pedestal sink and charcoal-finish faucet, both resembling contemporary sculpture. Geometric sconces maintain the gallery effect, as does a framed silver-gelatin print.

side show

It's all about the sink in this tight-fit powder room.

A custom concrete trough sink takes a minimalist approach while maximizing space in the 30×56-inch powder room of a Philadelphia townhome. "We put the faucet on the side, coming straight out from the wall, and it turned out to be an interesting solution to a small space," architect Christopher Beardsley says. Wall niches add storage and architectural interest to the windowless white room.

special effects

A soft, flowing curtain and mirrored surfaces work wonders in a remodeled room.

Powder rooms should be special, interior designer Richard Ross says. That notion guided him when remodeling this bath in a Michigan home. Ross and bath designer Jodi Caden, a member of the National Kitchen & Bath Association (NKBA), both worked on the space.

A dark, furniture-look vanity features mirrored doors that help visually enlarge the room. A sage-green curtain gracefully hides the toilet. "I like creating a little bit of drama," Ross says. "I wanted it to feel fresh, open, and still have privacy."

A bamboo wallcovering and pretty sconces add texture and warmth. "The room feels cozy and homey now," Caden says.

ABOVE LEFT: A satiny curtain serves as a partial wall, elegantly camouflaging the toilet. Mahogany flooring contributes a rich look.
LEFT: The marble counter keeps the room on the traditional side. Bamboo-covered walls, seen in the mirror, offer the same subtle patterns as the wood and marble. OPPOSITE: The large wall mirror and mirrored vanity doors visually expand the room. The frosted-glass door provides privacy without the mass of a solid door.

dream rooms, real budgets

4

Bathrooms are typically one of the first rooms a person steps into in the morning. So why not get your day off to a good start with a bath worthy of waking up to—and also one that helps you unwind at the end of a long day? The homeowners featured on the following pages did just that. Whereas they once had baths they simply tolerated, they now have ones they thoroughly enjoy—and they did it without endless budgets.

If you need justification beyond pure pleasure to commit to a makeover, consider this: an updated bathroom increases the value of your entire home. Even if you plan to do some of the work yourself, tapping a design professional before you jump in tends to be a good investment. A pro can help you make sense of a small space and offer advice on how you can shift things around or efficiently tap into existing plumbing. The ultimate goal is simple: your bath should be a feel-good space.

traditional treasure

A homeowner digs out the pretty photos she had clipped from decorating magazines and uses the ideas to turn her outmoded bath into a vintage gem.

Pink ceramic tile. A tub faucet that had to be turned on with pliers. A rickety toilet wedged next to the tub. Blue shag carpet. A goldenrod countertop and shell-shape sink. This bathroom had it all.

"It was so bad," homeowner Amber Siever says. "The only reason we used this room at all was to bathe the kids because the downstairs bath doesn't have a tub."

Amber and her husband, Bryan, had tackled other remodeling projects in their 1920s fixer-upper in Des Moines, but the upstairs bath stopped them in their tracks. In addition to the cosmetic problems, a corner closet at the head of the tub was virtually unusable because of its awkward location. The couple knew the room was going to need professional help.

OPPOSITE: Details such as the hexagonal tiles, cup pulls, and original vent cover keep this bathroom true to the look of the 1920s home.

LEFT: The flush-mount medicine cabinet, accented with a glass knob, looks similar to the original cabinet that was too worn to salvage. BELOW: Homeowner Amber Siever fell for this polished-nickel faucet the minute she saw it. She considered the old-world look and quality design to be an investment that would last for years. OPPOSITE: A neutral color scheme for classic elements such as the hexagonal floor tile, subway tile, and granite countertops gives the Sievers the option to change their color palette by painting the walls and swapping out the fabrics for a whole new look.

Although the room was small, Amber could see its potential from both a functionality and a looks standpoint—and she longed for the day she wouldn't dread going into it. She also knew she would have to be patient and have the less-glamorous work done before she could begin adding in the timeless touches that would make the room sparkle.

The Sievers hired a local construction company to make the bathroom work within its original footprint. The room was stripped down to the studs, and they started from scratch.

The remodeling project included new plumbing and wiring. Because of the age of the home, the floor had to be leveled and new plumbing lines installed, along with extra beams for structural support.

As part of the demolition, an unused closet was eliminated, and the tub took its place. That left just enough room for a toilet.

Subway tile adds retro flair to any room, but it's especially practical for a shower or tub area.

before

Inspiration Points

Homeowner Amber Siever used pictures she saw in decorating magazines to help her conceptualize and design her bathroom. She saved money by knowing exactly what products to shop for before the work began, and she got just the look she wanted.

Faucet

Amber had to convince her husband, Bryan, that this polished nickel model was worth the splurge.

Side table

This iron table was Amber's inspiration; she found a similar style on sale and loves how it personalizes her new bath.

Vanity

Amber favored this unit because of the two stacks of drawers and the illusion of feet at the toe-kick. She saved by giving up the curved front.

Mirror

A retro-style medicine chest was a near match for Amber's old one, which was beyond repair.

Amber knew what she wanted in a finished room. "I had four years' worth of pictures I had torn out of magazines." The magazine clippings served as a great tool for communicating ideas to the contractors. Glossy white subway wall tile and hexagonal mosaic floor tile brighten the room and create a distinctive foundation for this stylish and timeless look. The vanity, still in the same location as it was before the remodeling project, is a crisp white furniture-style piece with a dark granite countertop and undermount sink.

Amber longed to keep the built-in medicine cabinet above the sink, but it, like the rest of the bath, had seen too many years of wear and tear. She had the trim and cabinet removed and replaced with exact replicas. "My mother joked with us, asking why we were tearing everything out just to replace it with the same thing," Amber says.

The faucets turned out to be a conversation point for the couple. When Amber found the perfect traditional-style polished nickel faucets, Bryan balked at the price tag. "I thought it was absolute insanity to pay that much money for faucets," he says. But Amber recognized that the faucets would be the jewelry for the room and didn't want to settle. "We needed to invest in the fundamental things in the room for a timeless look," she says.

Polished chrome towel bars and sconces complement the faucets and give the formerly lackluster room her magazine-quality, finished look. "Now I tell people that the bathroom is the nicest room in my house," Amber says.

> **" I had four years' worth of pictures I had torn out of magazines. "**
>
> —HOMEOWNER AMBER SIEVER

ABOVE: **Clean lines from the white subway tile provide a timeless design. The gentle curves of the cap molding tiles create a graceful transition to the painted wall.** BELOW LEFT: **Towel bars shine against the soft gray-blue walls. They are an inexpensive way to freshen a bath.** BELOW: **The Sievers chose floor tile consistent with the original style of their 1920s home. The vanity has vintage-look hardware.**

patience pays

Plenty of time, smart shopping, and just enough color create a room with classic style.

THIS PHOTO: **Even though there's no window in this lower-level bathroom, the light color palette keeps it bright.** OPPOSITE: **Beaded board on lower walls adds to the room's crisp look.**

Stacy and Gavin Gaynor could have taken the quick route to a new bathroom in the lower level of their Saratoga Springs, New York, home. One shopping trip, and they might have been done. "But I wanted to avoid the look of a furniture showroom, where you bring home a packaged look," Stacy says. Instead they took their time, saving money and creating a distinctive, classic design.

The Gaynors lived in their home seven years before tackling the new lower-level bathroom project, and forethought saved them thousands of dollars. "We figured that at some point we would want to add a bathroom," Stacy says. So the couple had basement plumbing installed when the house was built.

They wanted the bathroom to be handy for family movie nights on the lower level. They also wanted a bath for overnight guests who stay in the adjacent room. So, with a disciplined approach to the project,

Stacy and Gavin listed everything they wanted in the bathroom, regardless of cost.

The wish list helped them identify their priorities when it came time for give-and-take. "I wanted a fully tiled shower," Stacy says. "But when I considered the cost, I realized I could have the look for less by tiling around a fiberglass shower insert. With the shower curtain drawn, you can't tell the difference." A glass shower door was nixed because of price. "As it turns out, I like the shower curtain better," Stacy says.

Patience can help a budget, too. "There are a lot of places where we felt we could save, but we didn't scrimp on labor," Stacy says. Despite their budget boundaries, they did splurge on marble floor tile—an eBay find that sets the casual elegant tone of the room. "It is amazing how much time you can devote to such a small space, but I am so happy we did. Our family and friends want to stay longer. I don't think you can put a price on that."

LEFT: Green accents in the shower curtain and a fern print create warmth. ABOVE: Open shelves provide just enough storage for guest amenities and accessories.

$ budget breakdown

- **PLUMBING**
  - Shower enclosure (including tile) — 920
  - Shower faucet and valves — 654
  - Sink, faucet — 889
  - Toilet — 649
- **SURFACES**
  - Flooring — 656
  - Paint — 50
  - Walls — 200
- **MISCELLANEOUS**
  - Labor — 8,000
  - Light fixtures (including fan light) — 300
  - Medicine cabinet — 2,316
  - Train-style towel shelf — 255
  - Shower curtain fabric — 90
  - Towel ring — 78

TOTAL — **$15,057**

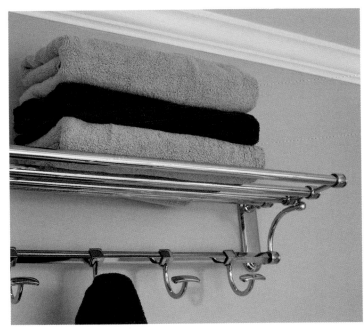

ABOVE: The towel rack is a replica of a design used on trains years ago to hold bags and coats. It adds a nostalgic touch to the bath. ABOVE RIGHT: Homeowner Stacy Gaynor chose a polka-dot fabric for piping and loops on the print shower curtain. RIGHT: A traditional faucet that evokes the same era as the pedestal sink reinforces the room's classic style.

The bath's color palette started with a colorful window treatment. The room boasts an organic feeling with a bit of a spa-like sensibility.

natural retreat

Taking a hall bath from blah to beautiful required careful planning and creative use of space. A designer employed both strategies to make this hall bath look pretty and live large. Then she added special touches to give it a soft, organic feel.

before

A few yards of fabric can launch the entire look of a room. Such was the case with the fabric that designer Jeni Wright chose for this bath's window shade. The fabric's color palette inspired the bath's sage wall paint and earthy tiles. To make the room look larger, Wright chose inexpensive field tile for the floor and installed it on a diagonal. Matching grout minimized joint lines, making the floor look like a single expanse of color. Next, she dressed the floor and tub surround with a more expensive glass border tile.

Coordinating iridescent tile in the shower shines in the natural light of the room. "The original archway into the shower was cute, but taking it out opened up the entire space," Wright says. Today a glass shower enclosure makes the room feel airy. "It allows natural light from the windows into the shower," she says.

In a small bath, carving out creative storage space is paramount. To do so, Wright built niches between the sink wall's joists, then added chunky wooden bases that extend the niches.

Between the storage niches, Wright replaced the original wall-mount sink with a sink cabinet for utilitarian storage. "In a small space, it's important to have great storage to keep clutter out of sight," she says. Above the sink, Wright opted for a flat mirror instead of a recessed medicine cabinet because there are electric and plumbing lines in the wall.

Other details also give the space a custom feel. A brushed-nickel sink and fixtures are the jewelry for the room. Invisible towel holders take the place of bulky shelving. Acrylic flowers floating on the wall mimic the pattern in the window-shade fabric. "The fabric is important because it's the only soft element in this room," Wright says. "Everything, right down to the flowers on the wall, had to be an extension of the fabric to achieve the cohesive, beautiful design."

ABOVE: Flowers raining down on the tub extend the fabric design into the rest of the room. ABOVE RIGHT: Using a glass half-wall allows natural light into the shower, making the room seem larger and more open. The iridescent herringbone tile inset adds a custom look.

Material Magic

A small swath of fabric covering a window is sometimes the only soft element in a bath, making it an important focal point and the driver of the room design. Here are some tips on how to use fabric as inspiration for outfitting a bath.

ACCENT COLORS Choose a wall color from one of the accent colors in the fabric.

TONAL RANGE Select accent colors in the same tonal range—not too light or too dark.

BACKGROUND COLOR Use the fabric's background color to determine trim color. If it's not pure white, avoid using pure white for trim.

DIMENSION Coordinate the fabric with accent tile. Its texture adds another dimension to the room's color scheme.

THIS PHOTO: **In keeping with her subtle color scheme, designer Jeni Wright chose a natural hue for the tub instead of bright white, which could have overpowered the room.**

Niches built into the wall provide an extra bit of storage space without taking up usable square footage.

before

budget breakdown

- CABINETRY
  - Vanity — 710
- PLUMBING
  - Sink — 136
  - Sink faucet — 463
  - Shower fixture — 250
  - Toilet — 315
  - Tub — 473
  - Tub faucet — 508
- SURFACES
  - Accent tile, field tile — 2,000
  - Countertop — 458
  - Shower glass — 1,169
- MISCELLANEOUS
  - Fabric — 155
  - Light fixtures — 68
  - Paint — 47
  - Toilet tissue holder — 78
  - Towel holders — 38
  - Wall flowers — 37

TOTAL **$6,905**

ABOVE: This fabric for the window shade drove the room's earthy look. BELOW LEFT: The thick wooden bases on the storage niches add a modern touch. BELOW: Stretch your tile budget by using a border made of decorative tile to perk up inexpensive field tile.

pure and simple

A mix of old and new elements transforms this master bath into a pristine beauty.

Like they did with the rest of their house, Molly and Jon Frey had to look past this bathroom's leaky roof and dark ceilings to see its potential. What it had the most potential for were headaches. But Molly, a former interior design student who started an architectural design business, looked forward to renovating the Massachusetts home. She and her husband, a commercial real estate investor, worked nights and weekends for two years to renovate their house. They saved thousands of dollars with Molly acting as the designer and Jon doing most of the labor.

Now complete, the master bath is one of the rooms they enjoy most. By stealing space from a small closet, they enlarged the bath, creating a private toilet room, an upscale feature often seen in new construction. They rearranged the room to allow space for a double vanity and a shower. A refinished antique table outfitted with plumbing fixtures is the new vanity, fitting snugly between two walls to ensure there's no wasted space. An old sliding barn door separates the bath from the adjoining master bedroom. Beaded board that runs horizontally makes the master bath look bigger and costs less than tile.

OPPOSITE: **An antique table was refinished to serve as a sturdy vanity. Classic vessel sinks and bridge faucets complete the clean cottage look.**

A sliding barn door ensures there's no space wasted from doors swinging into the room. Bonus: It adds a lot of character.

Though still small, the bathroom provides plenty of storage. Two recessed medicine cabinets store toiletries behind the mirrors. One comes complete with an outlet for a hair dryer. Tiny built-in niches behind the sink keep soaps and lotions at hand.

The enterprising couple made smart, cost-effective choices. Instead of replacing the floors, the Freys had the wide-plank pine floors stained ebony. The rich color visually anchors the white walls. With a little rearranging and innovate use of clever finds, the new master bath became a perfect combination of pure and simple elements.

$ budget breakdown

The Freys were able to keep costs down by doing much of the remodeling themselves.

- **CABINETRY**

Antique table (used as vanity)	900

- **FAUCETS/FIXTURES**

Faucets	1,000
Sinks	495
Shower fixtures	2,500
Toilet	330

- **MISCELLANEOUS**

Medicine cabinets	1,200
Glass for shower	1,100
Salvaged barn door	200
Hardware for barn door	450

- **TILE**

White subway tile	960
Tile labor	2,550

TOTAL	**$11,685**

LEFT: **Vessel sinks and nickel bridge faucets are reminiscent of an antique washstand.** OPPOSITE: **Instead of using a typical swing-out door, the homeowners opted for a salvaged sliding barn door.**

refresher course

Inspired by a candy-color tile, a homeowner gives her bathroom a clean-looking and eclectic makeover.

before

Do-It-Yourself Tips

FIND MEANING While creating a look you love, remember to include some elements that relate to the style of your home. Accessorize with colors and decorative items that are meaningful to you, keeping in mind the overall look and feel of the room.

STAY PUT Don't move or add plumbing if you don't have to. That's a major cost in a bathroom remodel.

SHOP AROUND Look for sinks, faucets, and vanities at home centers. You may be surprised at the array of styles you'll find. Compare the offerings from one store to the next.

SPLURGE SMARTLY Use expensive items, such as colorful glass tiles, as accents rather than entire backsplashes or walls. You'll save money, yet the room will still have impact.

LEFT: Touches of black ground the room and give the seafoam color more weight. In addition to providing practical storage, the new shelf displays some of the decorative knobs homeowner Katie Leporte collects. "They're like little gems," she says. OPPOSITE: Katie gave her bath a new look with a cool seafoam green theme and by accenting with artistic touches and both old-world and 21st-century details.

Katie Leporte wanted to redo her bathroom

but lacked inspiration. Then, one day, the magazine art director came across a seafoam green glass mosaic tile. That single small tile breathed new life into the bathroom in the Tudor-style cottage she shares with her husband, Mike, in Des Moines.

At work Katie had seen plenty of lackluster rooms transformed by homeowners who used a combination of sweat equity and old-fashioned ingenuity. She took her cue from that one glass tile and came up with a fresh and soothing look for her own bath. "I just really loved that little candy-color tile, and I wanted to make it work somehow," she says.

Katie was budget-conscious from the start. She didn't do expensive things such as moving plumbing lines and fixtures, though she did recruit her dad to help add a showerhead over the tub. "It's an old house, so all we had was a bathtub," Katie says. "I was tired of having to go down to my dark, dank basement to shower every morning."

With that big project done, her design strategy was simple: Focus on using little details that would have a big impact. Her husband, Mike, helped replace the bathroom's outdated laminate floor with white hexagon tiles that complement the home's classic style. For a dash of color, Katie bought a square-foot sheet of seafoam mosaic tile as an accent. "Then we just popped out every other white tile and replaced it with green," she says.

After scrubbing the tub to pristine condition, the couple had to protect the bathroom's only window from water damage. They sealed the existing window's woodwork with waterproof paint and topped it with a clear coat. Katie then made a curtain out of waterproof fabric to cover it. "Long-term, it's probably not the best option," she says. "But I think it will work for now, and it's not permanent, so we can change it later if we want to."

To ensure waterproof walls for the new tub-shower, the couple had to tear out the old lathe and plaster walls and put up waterproof cement board. To cut down on the expense of tiling the shower area, Katie took the seafoam tile around to home improvement centers and found the perfect match for less money. Again, she repeated the room's white and green scheme, using green square tiles as accents. "I just kept thinking, I have this one kernel of an idea and I need to build on it," Katie says.

Throughout the bathroom, Katie brought everyday things

to life with personal touches that added color and style. For the new white storage cabinet above the toilet, for example, she painted the knobs black and decorated each door with scrapbook paper designed by Amy Butler from Basic Grey. "It's my favorite scrapbook paper company," Katie says, adding that over time the papers have expanded from moisture so she plans to cover them with a paper sealer.

Katie created a display shelf beside the new sink by removing the door of an old, shallow built-in cabinet. After painting the shelves black and decorating the back with scrapbook papers, she drew a simple design on the wall and painted it with black acrylic. "I didn't want a stiff border," she says. "I wanted something unexpected, like it was growing right out of the shelf."

The whole look is an eclectic mix, Katie says, and she likes the way the classic beaded board contrasts with modern accessories, such as the towel bars and rings. "Those touches helped kick things up a bit. I didn't want Mike to think it's too girly," she says with a laugh. "Now I love my bathroom. It's such an improvement; I wish I would have done it sooner."

$ budget breakdown

CABINETRY, LIGHTING, MIRROR	
Base cabinet	310
Fixture over mirror	50
Mirror	45
Wall cabinet	40
PLUMBING & FIXTURES	
Sink, countertop	125
Sink faucet	50
Toilet	80
Plumbing for shower	260
SURFACES	
Accent tile, mosaic tile	90
Beaded board, molding	150
Field tile surrounding tub	110
Hexagon tile on floor	250
Paint	40
MISCELLANEOUS	
Hardware	15
Shower curtain	20
TOTAL	**$1,635**

modern angle

The sole bath in a 1950s ranch goes upscale and mod using a warm, neutral palette against angular shelves and gleaming surfaces.

THIS PHOTO: **Floating wood shelves hang behind a deeper and narrower unit with glass shelves, purchased separately.** OPPOSITE: **The palette contrasts neutral hues—dark brown and white—for pop and adds subtle blue-grays and silvers, avoiding colors that could date the look.**

THIS PHOTO: A geometric vanity and bowl sink carry a warm, brown hue across different materials for a cohesive look. OPPOSITE: The bathroom's original '50s layout wisely uses the shower wall to hide the toilet from view upon entry.

Minimalism has no price tag, although its sleek, perfect surfaces and exacting geometry are often synonymous with high-style, high-budget construction. Or so reasoned Karin Edwards, who had a spare, sophisticated look in mind to upgrade the tiny bath in her 1950s flat-roof home in Des Moines.

"This was a starter house when it was built and it remains one for me, but there's no reason it has to look that way," Karin says. Nevertheless, she knew that giving her bath a high-style look on a limited budget would be a challenge.

The bones of the bathroom were not half-bad. "It was kind of clever," Karin says. The tub was roomy and interestingly shaped, and the toilet was tucked out of sight behind the shower stall. Previous owners put in a laminate floor and installed a pedestal sink. The design was nice, but not practical. "It was cute, really cute—a white sink with a tilting mirror over it and beaded board everywhere. That just wasn't the direction I was going," Karin says.

Style preferences aside, added storage had to be part of the solution. (The former owners relied on an armoire in the hallway to hold some of the things the tiny bathroom could not.)

Karin mounted a modern angular shelving unit to the wall beside a matching vanity and mirror. She found the three pieces marked down at a local bath showroom at such a good price, she bought them all without even measuring. "It took me two years to save for the bath renovation, so I stored them in my garage in the meantime," she says.

Even though the proportions of these pieces weren't perfect for the space, Karin knew she could make them work. Stained dark brown, they proved a good-enough match to two floating wood shelves she picked up in a home store. Much longer, and much shallower, the added shelves created a new geometric form when mounted off-center to the shelving unit and, in the process, helped bridge the awkward space between it and the sink cabinet.

"It's a small, boxy room without distinguishing architecture. It needed some type of geometric form for interest," Karin says. "Plus, the strong horizontals help visually enlarge the space."

Illusion was key to the design, especially after the ceiling height dropped. Once topped with exposed beams painted white for a cottage look, the room now features a lower drywall ceiling that incorporates

" Tiny nooks have to multitask. What works as a shower seat in this stall doubles as elbow room during long soaks. **"**

—HOMEOWNER KARIN EDWARDS

LEFT: The raw salvage edge on this valance looks like fringe and offers a ready-made border that picks up on the rich texture of grass cloth on the walls. OPPOSITE: Resurfacing the square tub's porcelain from fleshy pink to white proved a cost-savvy update and preserved a versatile design.

Luxury Looks for Less

THINK RICH Dark stains add a sense of depth and character to the plainest wood grains and are easier to match than lighter hues when mixing the different woods of bath furniture gathered over time.

GO MOD Modular bath furniture offers freedom of placement, allowing an assemblage of store-bought pieces to masquerade as custom built-ins that suit your individual needs.

LEAVE SPACE Nothing says luxury more than plentiful space. In tiny rooms, leave one wall free of cabinets and decoration. Even if all other walls are jam-packed with cabinets and extras, this open expanse will function as breathing room to visually enlarge the space.

recessed lighting. "I considered how many weekends it would take to strip the ceiling paint, and I thought, *Well, this is a really good time to also improve the room's lighting,*" Karin says.

The ceiling's added expense was no budget stretch, because Karin was able to keep the existing square tub. Set on a diagonal, it offers ample elbow room to soakers. But its fleshy pink color had to go, so she had it reporcelained white and surrounded with a basic white, low-cost tile for bright counterpoint to the dark-stained furniture in the room.

With a grass-cloth wallcovering added for subtle color and shiny nickel and chrome accessories for accent, the bathroom slowly evolved into the little treasure box Karin envisioned. "It's soft, warm and edgy all at the same time," she says. Best of all, her elegant redo cost less than $2,000.

$ budget breakdown

- **FIXTURES**
  Bathtub refinishing   175
  Vessel sink   150
  Sink faucet   150
  Sink cabinet base   300
- **HARDWARE & LIGHTING**
  Recessed ceiling lights   120
  Mirror   125
- **WALLS**
  Wallcovering   270
  Tile   85
  Shelving unit   200
  Floating shelves   75

TOTAL   **$1,650**

splash of glamour

It started with wallpaper. But eventually a complete redesign turned this narrow, plain-Jane bath into a getaway reminiscent of 1940s Hollywood.

THIS PHOTO AND OPPOSITE: Pretty accessories gracefully finish off this guest bath. Reflective surfaces help bounce light around the narrow space, making it seem larger.

before

When homeowner Jan Kuttnauer of Atlanta was looking to update her guest bath, designer and friend Sherry Hart suggested adding wallpaper for a quick refresher. But wallpaper quickly led to new flooring, some furniture, and accessories, too. Framed Alberto Vargas prints of pinup girls further inspired the design with its shiny surfaces and black-and-white decor, a nod to the playful and glamorous Hollywood of the 1940s.

Hart found the grass-cloth paper, and Jan knew it would be perfect. It flowed with the rest of the home's feel, and it was subtle enough for the small space. But after assessing the rest of the bath, they could see that the wallpaper belonged with better company. "It went from wallpaper to, 'Well, while we're at it, we might as well do this,'" Hart says. "It was like a domino effect." She couldn't let such chic wallpaper go unsupported, so she began looking for other upgrades.

The vanity was the next big consideration. The challenge was to find one that fit the narrow room and had the stone countertop and open shelving Jan wanted. Hart had a vanity custom-made—at about the same price as in-store models—to fit the width restriction and include Jan's requests.

But like the wallpaper, the vanity led to more upgrades. The new vanity conflicted with the original floor and wall tiles, so Hart snagged some Calcutta gold marble on sale. The 18×18-inch pieces were cut in half and laid like subway tile. Tiling partway up the wall in the vanity area keeps the small space looking uniform and uncluttered.

To make the room appear larger, Hart again went custom and had a mirror that spans the vanity wall cut on-site. The reflective wall keeps the room light and bright. Deco-inspired shaded light fixtures installed on the mirror add an extra layer of sparkle, as well as illumination. "The mirror and lights certainly add the glam touch we were going for," Jan says.

Other little touches add to that old Hollywood aesthetic. Jan's favorite is the custom shower curtain, which puts a modern twist on an overall black Moroccan tile pattern on white. Wall art picks up the black and white tones as well.

The Plexiglas dressing table was a practical addition with a lot of style. It creates a second area for primping, away from the vanity and sink. "It fits into that Hollywood glamour, and it's translucent so it looks like it's not taking up much space," Hart says.

This guest bath makeover wraps up a long list of renovations Jan and Hart started seven years ago. "Now the house is perfect," Jan says. "Well, except the laundry room. That's next."

ABOVE: The Plexiglas dressing table, positioned for natural light, was a genius way to add a functional piece without visually taking up space. "It is the perfect spot for applying makeup and doing your hair," Jan says. An upholstered stool adds a bit of softness, as do floor-to-ceiling drapes.

$ budget breakdown

- CABINETRY
  Vanity   1,300
- PLUMBING
  Sink, faucet   535
- SURFACES
  Countertop   300
  Flooring   1,863
  Wallpaper   773
- MISCELLANEOUS
  Dressing table   600
  Light fixtures   430
  Mirror   700
  Stool   120

TOTAL   **$6,621**

RIGHT: A shallow vanity that squares out to accommodate the sink suits the small room. The open design, which includes shelves, ensures that the room isn't boxed in.

BELOW: Grass-cloth wallpaper is a perfect companion to the natural cedar sauna, which is original to the 1952 house.

Pick the Right Paper

Wallpaper is an inexpensive and easy way to add drama to a bath. Designer Sherry Hart shares her tips for choosing it.

GO NEUTRAL Neutral wallpapers are ideal for small spaces such as powder rooms or cozy baths. They make a room appear larger and complement any color of towels or bath accessories.

ADD INTEREST A solid color looks best if it is textured. Texture creates interest, even if the paper is painted over.

JAZZ IT UP Trendy wallpapers—geometry and nature motifs—are an effective way to instantly modernize a bath.

CONSIDER SCALE Pattern size is important. If you use a large pattern in a small space, you could lose its impact.

BE SMART Inexpensive wallpaper is your best bet in everyday or nonventilated baths because of water and steam wear. A less water-resistant paper should be used only in powder rooms and infrequently used baths where humidity is not an issue. You wouldn't want to use a very pricey paper in a bath that might be really steamy.

unfitted charm

An architect shares his secrets for transforming a basic bath into a haven with historical charm.

THIS PHOTO: **Salvaged items, including medicine-cabinet doors made from old shutters and a vanity base made of thick iron fencing, give this bath a vintage look.** OPPOSITE: **White vessel sinks pop against the limestone countertop.**

LEFT: Weathered interior shutters get a new life as doors to the recessed medicine cabinet. The original hardware is centered between the joined shutters, but the door still swings open from the side. A mirror is installed on the back side of the shutters.

old bath in need of a facelift," Jones says. He created a focal-point vanity from a piece of salvaged iron fencing, which he had welded to an iron frame to support the counter and sinks. New limestone covers the top. "Natural stone brings a centuries-old appeal," Jones says. New vessel sinks add elegance and are reminiscent of old washbasins.

Medicine cabinets recessed into the walls on both sides of the vanity hide behind eye-catching heirlooms—old interior shutters that were cut to door size. Vintage-style subway tiles cover the shower and bath walls. The flooring in the master bath is new ceramic tile that replicates a classic pattern in black and white marble.

Above the shower and vanity, wide crown molding matches the size and pattern often found in old bungalows, as do the four-pane double-hung windows inside the shower and above the vanity.

"I am a coveter of old items," Jones says. "If there is a way to make salvaged materials a functional and beautiful part of an interior design, I will find it."

Most remodeling projects make a room look new. Not this one. What Joe McGinnis enjoys most about the remodeled master bath in his Atlanta home is that it looks old. Like the rest of the home, it has charm. The secret? Salvage!

Joe discovered his home by accident. "One day I drove by, and there was a for-sale sign in the yard. I stopped, knocked on the door, and was told the home just sold. I was disappointed, but fortunately for me, that sale fell through and the owner called to see if I was still interested. I bought it the next day."

Because the original owner, residential designer Jeff Jones, had done so much attractive design work to the house, Joe had to do little more than move in and start enjoying the rewards of Jones's good taste. "From both inside and out, you would never know that this is a newer home," Joe says.

Nowhere is that old-home ambience more evident than in the master bath. "The finishing touches I applied to the master bath can be used to make over any bath, whether it's in a new suburban home or an

Building Character

Giving a new bath an old look isn't as difficult as it may seem. Just put on your thinking cap and start looking around for diamonds in the rough.

BE A SLEUTH Scour salvage yards for sinks, bathtubs, and other vintage pieces. A Habitat for Humanity ReStore is also worth checking out .

FAKE IT If you're not a period purist, reproduction sinks and faucets are great way to add character. When shopping in a store, ask if you can purchase a floor model at a reduced price.

REPURPOSE Think about how an item could be used in a new or different way. Look around your attic and your relatives' attics for a vintage piece that could be retrofitted into a vanity or storage hutch. If just the top of one piece of furniture is in excellent shape, consider adding it to the bottom of another piece.

ABOVE: The combination of salvaged fencing for a vanity base and salvaged wooden shutters for medicine cabinet doors gives the bathroom vintage charm. LEFT: Because a shower is a wet area, architect Jeff Jones had the wood window frames painted with marine-quality enamel. But Jones says, "The windows are high enough that water hasn't been a problem." BELOW: The key to making a vanity from an old iron piece is to make sure it doesn't look like a section of contemporary fencing; the heavier and more ornate it is, the better.

skimming the surface

By keeping some features she loves, this homeowner fashions a new bath without all the full-blown remodeling headaches.

ABOVE: **Subway tiles take the combination tub and shower up a notch, giving it a spa-like quality.** OPPOSITE: **Keeping the existing floor plan and simply upgrading old fixtures gave homeowner Nelle Kottman the updated look she wanted on a budget.**

Thirty years ago, when Nelle Kottman's house was built, two young children staked claims to the hall bath every morning. With the kids grown and gone, Nelle decided the bath needed to grow up, too. So the home improvement TV show junkie put together a design plan. Because the wallpaper and floor were in good condition, Nelle saw no need to replace them. Instead, she designed around them. "I have a thing for stripes and wanted to keep those," she says. The vertical lines of red and bisque on the walls add a sense of height.

Nelle also kept the vanity, giving it new life with a fresh coat of paint and new hardware. She replaced the old laminate

countertop with solid-surfacing for an upscale look and smooth, silky feel. A modern drop-in sink and faucet complete the vanity's new look. The mirror was original to the room, but Nelle updated the look by having it cut from a large rectangle into a circle with a beveled edge.

Upgraded plumbing fixtures add more style. Their bisque color matches the background of the wallpaper and the freshly painted vanity. Because Nelle doesn't have a tub in her master bath, she added a deep, jetted tub for days when she wants a leisurely soak. The old tub/shower surround was a molded enclosure. For an upgraded look, Nelle selected tan subway tiles to surround the shower area. A row of shimmering accent tile adds a bit of sparkle. To complete the suite of bisque fixtures, she opted for a new toilet, too.

Nelle incorporated built-in niches into the shower surround for extra storage. The ceiling fixture mimics the look of handblown Italian glass in an inexpensive version from a home center. "I didn't need a $500 light fixture," Nelle says.

Now, from the ceiling to the floor, Nelle still has the striped wallpaper she's enjoyed for years with the updated look she'd been imagining. "I just love this bathroom," she says.

RIGHT: **A subway tile surround adds upscale style. The jetted tub makes for a relaxing end to a long day.**

$ budget breakdown

- CABINETRY
  - Hardware — 300
- PLUMBING
  - Shower system — 749
  - Sink faucet — 268
  - Sink — 520
  - Toilet — 511
  - Tub — 2,900
- SURFACES
  - Countertop — 1,005
- MISCELLANEOUS
  - Light fixture — 40
  - Mirror cutting — 230
  - Paint — 185

TOTAL — **$6,708**

Making a Splash

Nelle Kottman used smart ideas to pack personality into her small hall bath.

INCORPORATE STORAGE Get creative to stretch storage in a small space. In Nelle's bath, niches in the shower enclosure hold soaps and shampoo.

ADD TEXTURE Subtle texture appears throughout this bath. From sleek subway tiles to the gentle weave in the shower curtain to the fluffy towels and the sailcloth valance, the room has a nice mix of tactile surfaces.

EMBRACE COLOR There's no rule that says a small space has to be neutral. Nelle kept the red-striped wallpaper she loved and brought in its subtle background color in fixtures and finishes.

INCLUDE TAILORED TOUCHES A crisp, pleated window valance adds a clean look with a touch of softness without blocking natural light.

ABOVE RIGHT: **The adjustable shower wand and grab bar provide ease of use. The brushed nickel finish adds an upscale touch.** RIGHT: **Niches built between wall studs add convenient storage in the shower.**

freshen up

A bath stuck in the '80s gets a modern look thanks to smart shopping and a we-can-do-it attitude.

THIS PAGE AND OPPOSITE:
Soothing color and warm wood tones make this bath seem like a contemporary spa retreat.

before

Kate and Dave Malo cut their remodeling teeth on the hall bath of their 1950s ranch home in Ankeny, Iowa. The bath, remodeled in the '80s, needed an update. Kate, a magazine graphic designer, spends her days surrounded by images of beautiful baths. She made mental notes, kept manila files of inspiration, teamed up with her handy hubby, and created a bathroom reflective of her desire for a modern and elegant style.

With advice from both of their dads, the couple set out to create a contemporary space on a budget—doing all the work themselves. They bought nearly all of the fixtures needed to do the job at a home center. Opting to keep the original bathtub and window allowed them to spend more on things that mattered most to them: flooring, tile, vanity, and toilet.

Their work began with demolition. "The room was cut in half by faux-tile paneling. It needed to be one solid color to feel larger," Kate says. They tore the paneling out, along with the tub surround. "When we started tearing things down, I had a split-second thought wondering if we could do this," Kate says.

Committed, they installed sage-green mosaic glass tile around the tub. They retextured the rest of the walls and painted them in a coordinating green for a cohesive look.

Then the couple tested their mettle on flooring, another project new to them. They wanted wood to coordinate with the rest of their home, but ultimately chose bamboo for its durability and modern flair. The new vanity the couple installed defines the room's contemporary look with its open design and sleek faucet. "The vanity is modern, but still warm because of the rich wood tone," Kate says.

That sleek styling, however, meant a decrease in storage capacity. To compensate, they used baskets to organize an existing closet. "We used the closet before, but without the organization, it wasn't as functional," Kate says.

ABOVE: **Inspired by shelves she saw at a posh retail store, homeowner Kate Malo had budget-friendly pine versions made. To save more money, she painted—rather than stained— them dark brown to match the wood in the room.**

LEFT: The modern sink and vanity launched the room's clean, linear look. BELOW: The open vanity has the storage functionality of a closed cabinet. Handy drawers hold wash cloths, hand towels, and soaps. Baskets on the shelf partially hide bath salts and sponges. Running the grain of the bamboo floor the length of the room makes the space seem larger.

Custom Look on a Budget

MIRROR AN IMAGE If you can live without the storage, skip the standard-issue medicine chest and make a statement with a framed mirror. The larger the mirror, the more light and color it reflects. Frames add a custom look, as well as heft that establishes the vanity area as a focal point.

GET THE COLOR RIGHT Paint is one of the least expensive ways to get big impact. Homeowners Kate and Dave Malo originally painted the bath a pale green. But the mellow hue didn't add depth. So they repainted with a color that links all the shades of green.

FACTOR IN FABRICS A custom window shade and shower curtain give this bath an upscale look, and allowed Kate to choose from a wide range of fabrics. If you can't sew, check fabric stores for a list of people who can.

BE ART SMART Although often overlooked, art is an easy way to finish off a bath. Kate simply printed initials on her computer, then matted and framed them.

"We wanted to create a space that was casual but elegant and reflected our personal style."

—HOMEOWNER KATE MALO

LEFT: **Baskets efficiently organize the narrow closet. They eliminate clutter and can be pulled out to tote the contents to wherever they will be used.** OPPOSITE: **Various shades of green unify the bath and make the small space seem larger. The mix of patterned fabrics creates visual interest.**

before

The increased organization also allowed them to ditch the medicine cabinet in favor of an oversize mirror framed in matching wood. A traditional light fixture mounted above it adds a pleasing note of contrast.

Continuing the contrast, Kate paired two patterned fabrics in coordinating colors. A traditional all-over diamond and floral pattern is on the custom Roman shade, while a modern stripe appears on the shower curtain. The shower feels roomier because of the curtain rod curves.

Putting their official stamp on the room, Kate designed custom art with their initials to hang on the wall. "It's ours," she says. "We did it as a couple, and the biggest compliment we get is when people see it and say, 'It looks just like you guys.'"

$ budget breakdown

▪ HARDWARE & LIGHTING	
Mirror	125
Vanity light	75
▪ PLUMBING FIXTURES	
Sink	190
Sink faucet	150
Toilet	120
Vanity base	470
▪ SURFACES	
Bamboo flooring	140
Tile	800
TOTAL	**$2,070**

better with age

Salvage finds—from flooring to fixtures to a tin mirror frame—bring character to a guest bathroom.

THIS PHOTO: **A hall bath evokes a serene feeling by using an antique tub and an old table repurposed for the vanity. On the wall, salvaged faucet handles serve as hooks. Knotty pine floors were salvaged from a 200-year-old warehouse.**

OPPOSITE: **An old wooden bowl used as a soap dish suits the salvaged theme.**

A well-appointed room resembles a top-ranked boxer in the ring: elegant and graceful, demonstrating an apparent lack of effort while making sure-footed design "punches." The guest bathroom in Joe McGinnis's Atlanta home is one such knockout.

The modest-size space sits off a long central hallway on the home's main level; the house was built in 1996 but was inspired by 19th-century floor plans. The bath's high-profile location meant that every design decision had to be carefully considered so every element looked as though it has always been part of the home—or at least didn't look like it had come straight off a shelf at a design center.

An antique French wood console table converted into a vanity carries the makeover. It's complete with an oversize vintage drop-in sink and a soap dispenser. "The table is large enough that it's really functional for cleaning up," Joe says.

Above the sink, a mirror framed in salvaged tin is still adorned with peeling paint. The mirror's oversize scale allows it to function as both reflecting surface and

ABOVE: **High ceilings create an open atmosphere, and a large window brings in lots of natural light. Vintage furnishings include the large antique mirror frame, the table that serves as a vanity, and the old sink.**

focal point, and its antique style reinforces the decor in the rest of the house.

A freestanding tub—another salvage yard find—was reglazed and updated with a rain-style showerhead and spare, neutral-color linen shower curtains. At the foot of the tub, a small slab of marble serves as a shelf for soaps and other bathing necessities.

Underfoot are knotty pine floors reclaimed from a warehouse in Pennsylvania. Antique hot and cold knobs from an old tub found new life, repurposed as hooks for towels and robes. A curvy toilet—old-school in looks but outfitted with modern water conservation features—rounds out the room.

Joe, a stylist and an editor, continues to adjust the bath's small accents, such as glass bottles and soap trays. But the style remains true to ready-for-the-ring form. "I always want every space to be ready for an impromptu photo shoot," he says.

RIGHT: Double-glazed and in mint condition, the vintage oval sink looks like a new drop-in model. A curved faucet completes the look.

$ budget breakdown

▪ CABINETRY	
Vanity	500
▪ PLUMBING	
Faucet, sink	50
Tub	1,200
Showerhead	65
▪ SURFACES	
Flooring	500
▪ MISCELLANEOUS	
Crown molding	200
Mirror, frame	500
TOTAL	**$3,015**

Recycle Your Remodel

REDUCE One of the most powerful ways to green up any remodeling project is to minimize waste. Go gentle with the demo work, and try to find new homes for items that are still in good condition.

REUSE As this bath shows, using salvaged items creates a one-of-a-kind look that's kind to the environment. Take the concept a step further. Use leftover paint from the project to spiff up a small room elsewhere. Turn scraps of lumber into a shelf or trim on a mirror.

RECYCLE Make sure all eligible waste is recycled—responsibly. Check with your local waste authority if you have questions.

worth the wait

Low-cost remodeling transforms every inch of this 1960s bath.

before

Randy and Julie Wenger didn't realize they had saved the worst for last. But after years of updating other parts of their Overland Park, Kansas, house, they finally focused on the 5×12-foot hall bath and discovered they had their work cut out for them.

"When we tore out the cabinet and flooring, I knew that the floor had rotted," Randy says. Water was also the reason the window above the tub was in disrepair. The frame was speckled with rust and trimmed with wood so moisture-ridden it wouldn't accept paint.

To launch their drier and better-looking bath, Randy and Julie chose mosaic stone tile for the floor. They repaired the original subfloor, then installed cement board before tiling to avoid future water damage and eliminate any shifts that could cause cracks.

OPPOSITE: **Nearly everything in this outdated bath was replaced. The tub was economically refinished by a professional. A home center offered many of the room's solutions—from a moisture-resistant window to vinyl wainscoting.**

White ceramic tile protects the shower walls, while vinyl wainscoting that mimics the look of beaded board provides a waterproof surface on the remaining walls. "I've joked that if you shut the door you can fill the whole room with water clear up to your waist," Randy says.

He found a dry solution for the window, too: the replacement is a vinyl-clad unit. Randy tiled up to it, installed the trim on top of the tile, and caulked well.

"Once it was done," says Randy, "we loved it so much we thought, why didn't we do it years ago?"

before

ABOVE: The homeowners swapped the original vanity for a narrower, furniture-style piece they found at a home center. The dark wood cabinet has drawers for toiletries and a shelf for towels. A matching mirror completes the look.

$ budget breakdown

Randy and Julie Wenger splurged on tile and saved by shopping a local home center and handling much of the basic labor themsleves.

- TILE
Floor and shower tile	1,500
Tile installation	800
- CABINETRY & PLUMBING
Vanity and sink	500
Showerhead	145
Sink faucet	90
- LIGHTING
Lighting	250
- MISCELLANEOUS
Wainscoting, wallboard, trim, and paint	500
Tub refinishing	400
Custom-size window	400
Mirror	100

TOTAL	**$4,685**

ABOVE: A vinyl window with a sliding sash replaced the moisture-prone wood-framed casement. The simulated divided light design mimics the rest of the home's windows. Unlike the original tile, the new subway tile extends above the window frame and showerhead to protect the shower walls. ABOVE RIGHT: This centerset faucet is a good choice for a vanity without much room behind the sink. An undermount sink provides maximum counter space and makes wiping up spills on the marble countertop easy. RIGHT: Mosaic tile in three shades of marble is the bath's most dramatic element and establishes the color palette. Though the basket-weave pattern looks intricate, the tile comes in 12×12-inch mesh-mounted sheets for simple installation.

bath
workbook

5

Planning a bath is like being in school—you have to do the homework. Choosing a vanity, flooring, tile, and other elements can be overwhelming. Do you want a natural wood or painted vanity? Should you go with a self-rimming sink or a sculptural vessel that sits on the vanity countertop? Have you decided on ceramic tile or will you splurge on sparkling glass mosaics? This guide will lead you through the decision-making process.

As you study up on the options and set your budget, be prepared to call in some professionals. If you're thinking of a jetted tub, for example, you'll need to make sure your floor can support the weight when it's filled with water. If you're thinking of switching the location of fixtures, a plumber can access ways to most efficiently tap into plumbing lines. The bottom line? A little pre-planning and diligence will move you one step closer to acing your bath remodeling project.

vanities

The vanity area is the centerpiece of your bath, so make it shine. Start with a vanity that sets the look and tone for the room—be it traditional or contemporary—and that will do justice to all the little pretties you put on and around it. In a small bath, the vanity may be the only storage option you have, so consider functionality, too.

Good to Know

STYLES Traditional cabinet-style vanities offer the most storage, keeping items together in drawers and behind doors. Furniture-style vanities set on legs are a fashionable alternative to traditional cabinets, as are consoles, which tend to have open shelves in their lower areas. While both styles give a small bath some visual breathing room, nothing does that quite like a wall-mounted vanity. These clean-lined contemporary vanities appear to float, giving a room an airy look.

HEIGHT Avoid back-aching stoops to reach your sink bowl by choosing a right-height vanity. The 30-inch height is becoming a thing of the past. For most people, a 36-inch-tall vanity and countertop combination is preferable. This height is similar to the work surfaces in a kitchen.

BUYING OPTIONS A stock vanity is the least expensive—just go to a home center and pick one out. Sizes and colors are limited, though. The next step up is semicustom cabinetry. This is also factory-made and comes in standard sizes, but offers more options in finishes, features, and materials. Allow several weeks, or even a few months, of lead time for orders. If budget allows, a custom vanity can be a nice option for a small bath, since the unit is designed, built, and installed to fit a unique space.

QUALITY When you begin your search for the perfect vanity or other cabinetry for your bath, keep in mind that most cabinet boxes are now made using engineered-wood products such as medium-density fiberboard (MDF), particleboard, or

plywood. These products are veneered or laminated. Engineered-wood cabinets are less likely than solid-wood cabinets to expand or contract over time.

HARDWARE For a coordinated look, choose the same finish for vanity knobs and other finishing details, such as towel bars and light fixtures. Choosing items from within the same collection makes the shopping easy.

Natural wood: Consider the grain

Wood grain makes as much of a statement as the color. Compare the differences.

MAPLE

BIRCH

CHERRY

HICKORY

OAK

Door design: Choose your style

On a cabinet-style vanity, doors and drawers do the talking. Consider which door shape and type of insert works for the look you're after.

Shapes

SQUARE

ARCH

CATHEDRAL

SLAB

Inserts

RAISED PANEL

RECESSED PANEL

BEADED BOARD

DECORATIVE MOLDING

Vanity flair: A look at three popular styles

CABINET STYLE

A cabinet-style vanity offers the most storage. With full-overlay doors, this vanity has a clean look. Cabinets that sit on the counter provide additional storage.

FURNITURE LOOK

With rich wood and gracefully curved feet, this vanity resembles fine furniture. Setting a vanity off the floor just a few inches visually stretches the sight lines.

WALL MOUNT

The lightest look of them all, a wall-mount vanity seems to float. The look tends to be contemporary, though the materials can change the feel.

sinks and counters

A sink and countertop must star in function. But with today's wealth of styles and materials, they also play a big role in your bath's design. Start with the sink. To reduce installation costs, plan the sink location to take advantage of existing plumbing lines. Drop a new sink into or on a showy counter, and you'll have a feature that draws the eye, not just dirty hands.

Good to Know

Sink considerations

STYLE Sink designs have stepped up a notch, becoming functional pieces of art. Before you get swayed by looks, choose the installation type. A conventional self-rimming sink, where the basin drops into a cutout and its edges rest on the countertop, is the easiest to install. An undermount sink attaches below the countertop, hiding the rim and creating a smooth profile. Trendy above-counter sinks are where the more artful looks come in. These range from deep vessel sinks that look like bowls to shallow rectangular basins. Depending on the style and material, they take a bit more effort to keep clean or may not contain all splashes, which is why they're often used as statement pieces in powder rooms. Other sink options include space-saving pedestals and wall-mount sinks. The downside is there's no counter space.

MATERIALS Durability is a key consideration with sinks. Cast iron, usually coated with enamel, is heavy, durable, and easy to clean. Vitreous china, fireclay, and porcelain offer similar attributes. Acrylic, composite, and solid-surfacing have a stone look that's popular today, with less weight and seamless installation. A molded-through color hides chips and scratches. Metal, such as stainless steel, copper, and brass, can also be used in a sink. Consider the steel's thickness—the "gauge"—when shopping. The lower the number, the thicker and more durable the metal. If you're considering a glass sink, tempered glass is preferred to prevent cracks and shattering.

Countertop considerations

INSTALLATION The type of sink you choose will help narrow down your countertop selections. For an undermount sink, for example, you'll need a waterproof material such as granite, quartz, or solid-surfacing. Another option to consider is an integrated counter/sink. Because it's one continuous piece, there are no unsightly rims or crevices for bacteria.

MATERIALS Most baths don't have a lot of counter space, so a luxurious material isn't necessarily a budget-buster. Ask about granite remnants; you may be able to get a good deal on leftovers from someone else's project. Solid-surfacing, which is designed to look like natural stone, is also popular for baths. Nonporous, hypoallergenic, and easy to clean, it's a good option if you're concerned about mold or mildew. Sleek stainless steel and affordable laminate are easy-to-clean options. Tiles are another option, though keeping grout lines clean requires upkeep.

Glossary

ABOVE-COUNTER SINK
Sculptural basin that rises above the counter like an old-fashioned washbowl; also called a vessel sink.

CONSOLE SINK
Countertop surface, often with an integral basin, that rests on legs.

SELF-RIMMING SINK
Basin drops below the counter, its rim resting on the countertop; also called a drop-in sink.

FLUSH-MOUNT SINK
Sink rim rests flush with the countertop, with a metal rim bridging the two edges.

INTEGRAL SINK
Combines a countertop and a basin into one piece; usually molded of solid-surfacing or concrete or carved in stone or wood.

PEDESTAL SINK
Two-part fixture—a columnar base and a basin—that mounts on a bracket anchored in the wall.

UNDERMOUNT SINK
Sink mounts below the countertop so no rim or lip shows; the cutout is slightly smaller than the basin so the countertop overhangs a bit; also called a rimless sink.

WALL-HUNG SINK
Sink mounts to wall with special brackets.

faucets

A faucet is jewelry for the bath—a finishing touch that can be a sculptural focal point. When buying a faucet, consider how it is mounted, where its water stream will hit the sink bowl, and how it complements the sink and the room's decor. Buying a faucet and sink from the same collection is a foolproof way to get it right.

Good to Know

STYLE With a faucet, style and function go hand in hand. The faucet should suit the overall look of the room, but it also needs to work for your lifestyle. If you plan to wash hair in the sink, for example, you'll want a spout that's tall enough to allow for that or that has a pullout spout. Handle configuration is another consideration. A single-handle faucet makes it easy to regulate cold and hot water. Ergonomic lever handles that need no gripping or twisting are a boon for users with limited strength. As you shop, envision your routine and feel the faucet handles so you have an idea how they would operate.

FINISHES Durable chrome is a popular finish, but others are coming on strong. Brushed nickel, oil-rubbed bronze, and brushed copper are among the offerings.

Look beyond the color to how the finish is applied. A PVD (physical vapor deposition) finish is one of the most durable. Plating, such as chrome plate, is another indicator of durability; it helps protect against corrosion and tarnishing. Faucets with a "living finish," such as oil-rubbed bronze, will age and develop a patina over time. Moisture and cleaners can also change the look of these finishes.

COMPATIBILITY The number of holes in the sink deck or on the countertop will determine the type of faucet you can get. (See glossary, *right*.) But there are exceptions. Some faucets have a deckplate that covers the holes. So if your sink has three holes, you can actually still use a single-handle faucet, with the deckplate hiding the extra holes.

Glossary

BRIDGE FAUCET
Spout and handles linked by an exposed tube; can be deck- or wall-mount; traditional style.

CENTERSET FAUCET
Spout and two handles sit on a base, with handles 4 inches apart; affordable and good for tight spaces.

MIINI-WIDESPREAD FAUCET
Spout and handles are three separate pieces, but placed closer together than a widespread faucet; can replace a 4-inch centerset faucet; good for tight spaces.

SINGLE-HOLE FAUCET
Spout and a single handle in one unit; only one hole pierces the sink deck or countertop; also called post-mount faucet.

WIDESPREAD FAUCET
Spout and handles are three separate pieces, requiring a three-hole sink deck or countertop; distance between handles is between 6 and 12 inches.

WALL-MOUNT FAUCET
Spout and handles mount to the wall, from plumbing behind the wall; frees up counter space.

On-the-wall wisdom

Wall-mounted faucets are becoming popular—not just for their appealing look but for their ability to free up counter space and their cleaning ease. Here are a few things to ponder.

CONSIDERATIONS Above-counter sinks, especially bowl-style ones, typically require a wall-mounted faucet because conventional faucets tend to be too short. Wall-mount faucets require special in-wall plumbing instead of the typical under-the-sink location. Save room in the budget for the extra work.

FUNCTION When installed, the spout should be far enough above the sink rim to allow your hands to easily reach the water stream. A spout installed too high above the sink, however, can lead to splashing. A guideline: You need at least 1½ inches between the rim of the sink bowl and the bottom of the spout; 4–6 inches is average.

tiles

Walls, countertops, floors, showers, and tub decks—tile is everywhere these days, and with good reason. Tile is water-resistant, easy to maintain, and good-looking. Use neutral tiles for a spa-like look or create a sparkling backdrop with glass mosaics. The possibilities are endless.

Good to Know

CERAMIC The wide array of colors, shapes, and sizes is a hallmark of ceramic tile. The finish can be matte or glossy, giving you some flexibility in how much walls stand out. Ceramic is easy to clean, although grout may discolor. Price range: $2 per square foot, uninstalled, for basic ceramic tile; $8–$30 for upscale designs.

GLASS Surprisingly strong, glass tiles boast great color depth. They have a shimmering, liquid-look surface that reacts to light in a distinctive way. Glass tiles come in many colors, finish styles, sizes, and shapes, allowing one-of-a-kind looks. Glass tends to be the priciest tile surface. If budget is an issue, consider using it as an accent. Price range: Starting at $15–$20 per square foot.

METAL Striking and practical, metal instantly brightens a room. While steel lends a sleek and industrial look, warm metal tiles such as copper, bronze, and pewter contribute old-world charm. Metal

is impervious to stains but scratches easily. While some tiles are real metal, others earn the look from a glazed metal finish. Take note of the kind of tile you install before adopting a cleaning regimen. Most real metal tiles can be cleaned with gentle soap and warm water. Large doses of metal tile can be overpowering, so it's best used as an accent or as a backsplash. Price range: As low as 50 cents each for 1×1-inch metallic accent pieces and up to $100 each for handcrafted metal tiles.

STONE Natural stone tile such as granite, marble, and limestone is synonymous with luxury and offers a sense of permanence. With its neutral colors, it can make a bath seem like a spa. Stone works for most surfaces, from countertops and backsplashes to floors, tub decks, and shower walls. Stone is porous and can stain, so tiles need to be properly sealed. Price range: $4–$15 per square foot, uninstalled. Rarer stones can cost $40–$60 per square foot.

Glossary

BACKSPLASH
Protection of the wall at the back edge of the countertop; designed to seal the counter and protect the wall from spills and damage. Can be integral to the countertop or applied directly to the wall.

LISTELLOS
Decorative pieces usually installed as accent pieces or as a transition from one material to the next. Commonly referred to as border tiles. Can be expensive.

MOSAIC TILES
Small tiles generally ranging from ½x½ inch to 2x2 inches; 1-inch square tiles are most common. Tend to be available in sheets backed with netting that makes installation easier.

SUBWAY TILES
Rectangular tiles (often 4x6 inches); typically white or light-colored.

The big picture: Factor in grout

Choosing grout can be as important as selecting tile. You can achieve different effects depending upon the color you choose.

BLEND IN Select a grout color that closely matches the color of the tile to create a uniform look.

HIDE GRIME Dark-color grout hides dirt better than light-color grout, which can be difficult to clean.

STAND OUT To make tiles stand out, choose a grout color that contrasts with the tile, such as white grout against blue tiles. The contrast will emphasize the shape of the tile, drawing attention to it.

flooring

As one of the largest surfaces in a room, flooring naturally makes a big decorative impact. But choosing flooring goes beyond looks. A bath floor needs to be moisture- and water-resistant and not too slippery. Size up the choices to ensure the material you're considering is up to the task.

Good to Know

CERAMIC AND PORCELAIN Ceramic and porcelain tiles offer durability, as well as a wide range of colors, textures, and designs. Not all ceramic and porcelain tiles are rated for floor use, so make sure you ask before you buy, and opt for textured surfaces over glossy ones. Ceramic and porcelain tiles are easy to clean (though grout lines can be difficult), but are cold and hard on the feet. Price range: $8–$50 per square foot, installed.

CORK Eco-friendly cork resists moisture and germs and offers cushy comfort. Glue-down tiles make cork suitable for use in a bath, but it's still an unconventional choice. For maximum protection, seal the cork tiles with at least two coats of sealer, and caulk around the perimeter of the room to prevent water seeping into the subfloor. Be prepared to wipe up water immediately. Price range: $4–$9 square per square foot, installed.

GLASS One of today's hottest looks, glass mosaic tiles cover a floor (shower, too) in shimmering style. Glass tiles can be slippery to walk on, so ask for special options, such as a sandblasted surface that makes the tiles less slippery. Prices tend to start at $20 per square foot.

LAMINATE A tougher version of the plastic laminate used for countertops, laminate flooring can imitate wood, stone, or ceramic tile and offers unusual patterns and designs. Durability is good (though on low-quality laminate the top layer may peel from the core), and maintenance duties are light. Planks, strips, and squares glue or click together, often as a floating floor. Price range: $3–$10 per square foot, installed.

LINOLEUM Rich colors and patterns distinguish linoleum, which is made from natural raw materials. Available in sheets or tiles, linoleum repels dirt and resists bacteria. Solid colors and flecks are embedded throughout, rather than imprinted on the surface. It's more durable than vinyl, but it should be resealed annually and may scuff. Price range: $5–$9 per square foot, installed.

STONE Limestone, marble, granite, travertine, and slate make luxurious and extremely durable floors. Like ceramic and porcelain, stone is cold and hard on feet. Polished surfaces can be slippery when wet, so opt for honed tiles. Price range: $8–$50 per square foot, installed.

VINYL Dramatic visuals—stone, tile, wood, sisal, and more—combine with comfort and easy maintenance in today's vinyl offerings. It's also easy to maintain; just wipe up spills or splashes. Vinyl is less expensive than other flooring choices, but it's also difficult to repair. Look for it in tiles (including inexpensive self-adhesive squares for quick DIY updates) or sheets; 12-foot-wide rolls help avoid seams. Price range: $1–$7 per square foot, installed.

Special Touches

Floors are so much more than a space to walk across. Not only can they look good, they can feel good, too.

WARMING TREND To avoid cold floors—and cold feet—consider hydronic or electric radiant heat. Hydronic heating uses hot water forced through pipes laid under the floor. Electric radiant heating systems are mats installed above the subfloor and directly under the floor.

RICH LOOK Wood isn't typically recommended for a bath, but there are some varieties that are water-resistant. Teak, used in boats, and bamboo, an eco-friendly material, can provide a rich and unexpected look—and a warmer feel than tile. If you're considering wood, be prepared to wipe up water immediately.

PEBBLE PANACHE Bring the outdoors into your bath with a pebbled tile floor. Pebble tiles come in a wide variety of colors and textures, and the installation process is similar to ceramic tile. To get the look for less, confine the pebbles to a small area, such as a shower floor.

toilets

Often overlooked and underappreciated, the toilet may be the most important seat in the house. As you'll discover when you start shopping, there's more to modern toilets than pure function.

Good to Know

STYLE Still sold primarily in white or light neutral tones, toilet styles vary. Traditional two-piece toilets are still the most purchased models on the market. Sleek wall-mount toilets without tanks are showstoppers in contemporary baths. One-piece toilets offer a seamless look.

COMFORT Many manufacturers now offer toilets with seats set a few inches taller than the standard 14 inches. Taller toilets also work with universal design, allowing people with less mobility to sit and stand easier. Comfort also comes into play with the seat itself. Most people prefer the comfort of an elongated seat over a traditional round one.

ROOM FIT Toilets sizes vary, and an inch or two can make a big difference in a small space. Measure the toilet from its widest and deepest parts to make sure it will sit in your room without jutting into a doorway or your access to the tub. Consider the seat style, too. A traditional round seat occupies less space.

PERFORMANCE Flushing performance will ultimately make you either like or loathe your toilet. Compare models by talking to salespeople, checking online, and even asking friends who recently installed a new toilet. Bonus features—such as heated seats and remote-control lids—make shopping for a toilet a bit more fun.

Glossary

ELONGATED BOWL
Toilet is about 2 inches longer front to back than the standard round bowl.

LOW-FLUSH TOILET
Pressure-assisted or gravity-fed system that efficiently cleans the bowl using only 1.6 gallons of water; now the standard.

SELF-CLOSE SEAT
Toilet seat and lid have a special hinge that, with just a light push, lowers the seat to the bowl gently and quietly.

TANK
The toilet's reservoir for flush water; also called a cistern.

UNIVERSAL HEIGHT
Toilet seat is about the same height as the seat of a household chair for ease of use.

Toilet styles: A look at tank options

TWO PIECE
Two-piece toilets have a separate tank and bowl. They're traditional—though as this one shows, they can look sleek. On average, they are the least expensive toilet style.

INTEGRATED
One-piece toilets have an integrated tank and bowl design. They have a modern look and are generally more expensive than a two-piece toilet.

WALL MOUNT
Space-saving wall-mount toilets build the plumbing for the toilet bowl into the wall. The need for custom plumbing makes this a pricier option.

tubs and showers

Whether you love soothing soaks or invigorating sprays, there's a fixture that will suit your space and lifestyle. And it doesn't have to be an either/or choice. With a combination tub/shower, you get the best of both worlds.

Good to Know

Tub considerations

SIZE A standard tub is 5 feet long and 32 to 34 inches wide. Space and plumbing constraints may limit your options. Corner tubs can be a good solution in rooms with 48 to 60 inches open along adjacent walls. The ideal bathing well length lets you stretch out but braces your feet so you don't slide around. To compare tub shapes, nothing beats test-sits in a store.

MATERIALS Most tubs sold today are acrylic, which is sturdy and lightweight (60–70 pounds). Acrylic resists stains better than gel-coat fiberglass tubs, which are the least expensive. Weightier choices include porcelain-enamel on steel; budget-price models tend to chip and sound echoey. Enameled cast-iron offers a balance of price and durability but is extremely heavy. Tubs made of special materials, such as stone, copper, and teak, are also available—and expensive.

AMENITIES Jetted tubs deliver a vigorous massage; make sure all jets adjust in direction and force. The pipes need periodic flushing to clean them, though there are models with self-cleaning cycles. Soaking tubs offer an extra-deep bathing well; some people prefer that over jets.

INSTALLATION Have a plumber take a look at your room. The floor bracing must be able to support the weight of the tub, including when it's filled with water. Tapping into existing pipes from above, below, or an adjacent bathroom will reduce expenses. Before you buy a tub, measure it to make sure the tub will fit through doorways and stairways en route to your bath.

Shower considerations

AMENITIES If you're dreaming of a roomy shower, you may need to sacrifice the tub to get it. But even in a standard tub/shower combination, a tempered glass panel can make a shower seem larger. The right showerhead (or showerheads) can make even a small shower feel luxurious. The choices range from invigorating body sprays to gentle rains. (See glossary, *right.*) For flexibility, consider a handheld unit on a slide bar. It allows people of different heights to shower comfortably.

PLUMBING A powerful shower can be demanding on pipes and the water heater. Good water pressure—ideally 60–80 pounds per square inch (psi)—is key, even if you're just adding a rain showerhead. Otherwise, you'll get dribbles. To determine how much hot water you need, multiply the gallons of water per minute (gpm) the shower system uses by the time in minutes you tend to shower, then take 75 percent of the result. A typical 40- or 50-gallon water heater may not do the job for a luxury shower.

INSTALLATION The floor of the shower, called a pan, should have a slight rim to contain water and should slope toward the drain. The pan can be molded of synthetics, tiled, or carved from stone or wood. Walk-in showers should also have the floor sloped toward the drain.

Glossary

BODY SPRAY
Small water outlet set in the wall, positioned to spray a certain part of the body; high-end models adjust spray direction and intensity.

FIXED-POSITION SHOWERHEAD
Traditional showerhead attached to the wall; should be installed above the head of the tallest user.

FRAMELESS ENCLOSURE
Tempered-glass shower enclosure unit held together with discreet clips, translucent seam seals, and see-through drip guards for a nearly invisible look.

HANDHELD SHOWERHEAD
Showerhead connects to a water supply through a pliable hose; also called a handshower.

RAIN SHOWERHEAD
Large-diameter showerhead that holds many small spray nozzles; some models switch from relaxing rain-shower sprays to concentrated sprays.

THERMOSTATIC VALVE
Valve that compensates for a drop in water pressure on the hot or cold side to keep water within a safe temperature.

lighting

Choosing lighting for your bath is like planning an outfit. Just as the look improves with the layers, your bath benefits from several lighting types. Evaluate the room's size, shape, ceiling height, available natural light, and materials. Then put layers of lighting to work to ensure that the space you depend upon for grooming puts you in the best light.

Good to Know

OVERALL LIGHTING Every bath needs basic overall illumination, called ambient or general lighting. In small baths, one ceiling-mount fixture commonly supplies ambient lighting. (In tiny powder rooms, light from sconces or a bar strip above the vanity may suffice.) Make sure the light spreads into the shower so the enclosure doesn't seem like a cave. Depending on the size of the room, you may need to have a professional install a recessed ceiling light above the shower. Ambient lighting can't do everything, though. It's best to balance it with other types of lighting.

TASK LIGHTING As the workhorse of the room, the vanity area needs to be well-lit. Task lighting, which brightens a specific area or surface where tasks are performed, does the trick. Lights installed above or around the mirror should illuminate your face, not the mirror or even the ceiling. Task lights can also be incorporated into wall cabinetry or a custom medicine chest. Good task lighting should eliminate shadows and overhead glare, allowing you to groom effectively.

SAFETY CONSIDERATIONS Changing out the fixture above the vanity may be fine if you have some experience with wiring, but bigger jobs are best left to a pro. An electrician will know the electric codes (remember, electricity and water don't mix), can steer you to fixtures designed for wet areas, and will get the job done properly. Depending on the extent of your remodeling project, you may need to add or move electric outlets—something an electrician can tackle along with the light fixtures and switches.

Bright ideas: Ways to illuminate a bath

Windows and skylights earn bonus points in any bath, but you don't need natural light sources to make your room shine. Consider these ideas.

UPSIDE DOWN Many sconces and bar lights can be flip-flopped so globes point down rather than up. It's a nifty maneuver in a tight space, and it also directs the light down so you get more of it.

REFLECTION Think beyond bulbs to illuminate your bath. Reflective surfaces,

such as mirrors, shiny chrome faucets, knobs, towel bars, and glass or metal tiles bounce light around. Consider them a secondary light source.

CLEAN SCENE It's a given that globes will get dirty and bulbs will get dusty. But a clean bath equals a brighter bath—so simple!

Glossary

BEAM SPREAD
The area brightened by the light a fixture casts in a room.

CEILING-MOUNT FIXTURE
Provides general illumination from overhead; fixture is installed at the ceiling.

DECORATIVE LIGHTING
The fixture itself is the focus.

LAMP
Another word for bulb.

PENDANT
Hangs from the ceiling via a stem, wire, or cable to provide task and/or general illumination. In a bath, a pendant hung in the vanity area can add decorative flair.

RECESSED FIXTURE
Installs unobtrusively in the ceiling (only its bulb and lens are visible) to provide general and/or task lighting.

TRACK LIGHTING
Ceiling-mount electrified bar that houses movable and directional lights for task or accent purposes.

SCONCE
Decorative wall bracket housing a light; often hung on the sides of mirrors to illuminate the vanity area.

budget basics

Like any home-improvement project, a bath renovation is just as dependent upon practical financial calculations as it is on blueprints. Before you get too married to the idea of a jetted tub or glass mosaic tiles covering walls, crunch the numbers and set a budget. Then make your bath an oasis of comfort—knowing it's at a price you can afford.

Good to Know

NEEDS VERSUS WANTS Coming up with a budget will require you to spend some quality time distinguishing between the room's needs and your wants. Allow yourself plenty of brainstorming sessions to nail down your vision for the perfect bath, and then determine what parts of your current bath still fit into that vision and which ones need to be replaced. (See the worksheet, *right*.) Sometimes, a bath that is showing its age needs just a little polish, such as paint, new lighting, and cabinet hardware.

PERSPECTIVE Industry experts say a typical bath update costs from $7,000 to $12,000, which covers a new tub, sink, toilet, wall tiles, flooring, and lighting. Experts suggest homeowners will recoup 80 to 100 percent of those costs at resale time. However, keep in mind that a lavish bathroom renovation could boost the value of your home to the most expensive one on the street, which real estate professionals say generally will not help the marketability.

PROFESSIONAL HELP Working with a designer can be money well spent, especially if you're gutting the room and starting from scratch. A pro can help you avoid costly mistakes and know where to snare the best deals. He or she can also help refine your vision and offer ideas you may not have even thought about. If you can't afford to use a designer for all aspects

of the project, see if the person can provide an hour or so of consultation. When you meet with a professional—be it a designer, a contractor, or a plumber—have your budget in hand and be up-front about your finances. It doesn't do any good on either end if you fudge the numbers high or low. Don't hesitate to ask for client references. And when you talk with those customers, ask how well the professionals met their labor estimates. Expect the professional to visit your current bathroom before presenting an estimate; this eliminates costly surprises. After you receive that bid, add a 5–20 percent cushion to your budget to absorb unpredictable cost overruns, such as replacing drywall or tile grout that has absorbed moisture through the years.

BUDGET ALLOCATION Allocate your budget dollars after taking the time to shop around and discerning your needs from your wants. For products, here's one way to break down a budget: 40 percent for fixtures and faucets; 25 percent for cabinetry; 20 percent for flooring and countertops; 10 percent for overrun; and 5 percent for hardware. Shopping online saves time and lets you compare prices. But shop in person, too, so you can see the products you're considering. Things always look a bit different when they're right in front of you. Keep a detailed list of each product's features and price, and don't be afraid to ask if the product will be going on sale.

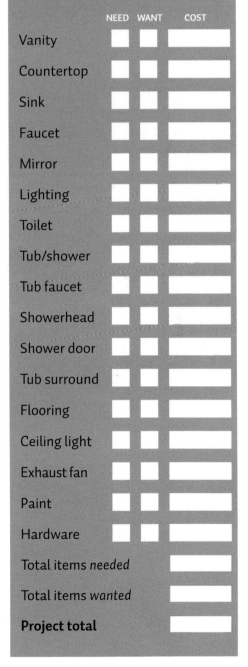

Budget Worksheet
Take stock of what you really need to make your bath functional. Also note those items that aren't critical to the project but are extras that would be nice—items you want.

	NEED	WANT	COST
Vanity			
Countertop			
Sink			
Faucet			
Mirror			
Lighting			
Toilet			
Tub/shower			
Tub faucet			
Showerhead			
Shower door			
Tub surround			
Flooring			
Ceiling light			
Exhaust fan			
Paint			
Hardware			
Total items *needed*			
Total items *wanted*			
Project total			

resources

cabinetry and vanities

AMERICAN STANDARD
800/442-1902
americanstandard-us.com

AMERICAN WOODMARK
800/677-8182
americanwoodmark.com

ARISTOKRAFT CABINETRY
812/482-2527
aristokraft.com

ARMSTRONG CABINETS
800/527-5903
armstrong.com/Cabinets

BATES & BATES
800/726-7680
batesandbates.com

DANZE
877/530-3344
danze.com

DIAMOND CABINETS
812/482-2527
diamondcabinets.com

JULIEN
800/461-3377
julien.ca

KLISE MANUFACTURING
616/459-4283
klisemfg.com

KOHLER
800/456-4537
kohler.com

KRAFTMAID CABINETRY
800/571-1990
kraftmaid.com

LACAVA LLC
888/522-2823
lacava.com

MARK CABINETRY
248/414-3568
cabinetryinc.com

MEKAL
905/602-6675
mekal.com.br

MERILLAT INDUSTRIES
866/850-8557
merillat.com

NATIVE TRAILS
800/786-0862
nativetrails.net

NEO METRO COLLECTION
800/591-9050
neo-metro.com

OMEGA CABINETRY
319/235-5700
omegacabinetry.com

PORCHER
800/359-3261
porcher-us.com

QUALITY CABINETS
972/298-6101
qualitycabinets.com

ROBERN
robern.com

RONBOW
888/880-8318
ronbow.com

SONIA AMERICA
888/766-4287
sonia-sa.com

STONE FOREST
888/682-2987
stoneforest.com

VILLEROY & BOCH
877/505-5350
villeroy-boch.com

WATERFALL
888/521-3141
waterfallbath.com

WATERWORKS
800/927-2120
waterworks.com

WELLBORN CABINET
800/336-8040
wellborn.com

WOOD-MODE FINE CUSTOM CABINETRY
877/635-7500
wood-mode.com

XYLEM
866/395-8112
xylem.biz

countertops

ALCHEMY GLASS & LIGHT
323/235-6606
alchemyglass.com

CAESARSTONE
877/978-2789
caesarstoneus.com

CAMBRIA
866/226-2742
cambriausa.com

DALTILE
800/933-8453
daltileproducts.com

DUPONT
800/426-7426
www2.dupont.com

ELKAY MANUFACTURING
630/574-8484
elkayusa.com

EVERLIFE STONE
800/627-8663
everlifestone.com

FORMICA CORP.
800/367-6422
formica.com

J. AARON CAST STONE
404/298-4200
jaaroncaststone.com

LG SURFACES
877/853-1805
lghi-macs.com

MEKAL
905/602-6675
mekal.com.br

**SILESTONE
BY COSENTINO**
800/291-1311
silestoneusa.com

SONOMA CAST STONE
877/283-2400
sonomastone.com

STARON SURFACES
800/795-7177
staron.com

VETRAZZO LLC
510/234-5550
vetrazzo.com

WALKER ZANGER
877/611-0199
walkerzanger.com

XYLEM
866/395-8112
xylem.biz

faucets
and fixtures

ALCHEMY GLASS & LIGHT
323/235-6606
alchemyglass.com

AMERICAN STANDARD
800/442-1902
americanstandard-us.com

AQUADIS
450/433-2210
aquadis.com

AQUATIC INDUSTRIES
800/555-5324
aquaticwhirlpools.com

**ARTISAN
MANUFACTURING**
973/286-0080
artisansinks.com

BARCLAY PRODUCTS
800/446-9700
barclayproducts.com

BATES & BATES
800/726-7680
batesandbates.com

BRIZO
877/345-2749
brizo.com

CAROMA USA
800/605-4218
caromausa.com

CIFIAL USA
800/528-4904
cifialusa.com

DAIEK PRODUCTS
daiekproducts.com

DANZE
877/530-3344
danze.com

DIAMOND SPAS
800/951-7727
diamondspas.com

DELTA FAUCET
800/345-3358
deltafaucet.com

DORNBRACHT USA
800/774-1181
dornbracht.com/en

DURAVIT
770/931-3575
duravit.com

ELKAY MANUFACTURING
630/574-8484
elkayusa.com

FRANKE
800/626-5771
frankeconsumerproducts.com

GRAFF FAUCETS
800/954-4723
graff-faucets.com

GROHE AMERICA
630/582-7711
groheamerica.com

HANSA
678/334-2121
hansa.us.com

HANSGROHE
800/334-0455
hansgrohe-usa.com

JACLO
800/852-3906
jaclo.com

JULIEN
800/461-3377
julien.ca

KALDEWEI USA
317/805-4822
kaldewei.com

KOHLER
800/456-4537
kohler.com

KWC FAUCETS
678/334-2121
kwc.us.com

LACAVA LLC
888/522-2823
lacava.com

LINKASINK
866/395-8377
linkasink.com

MEKAL
905/602-6675
mekal.com.br

MGS USA
561/218-8798
mgsdesigns.com

MOEN
800/289-6636
moen.com

MTI WHIRLPOOLS
800/783-8827
mtiwhirlpools.com

NATIVE TRAILS
800/786-0862
nativetrails.net

NEO METRO COLLECTION
800/591-9050
neo-metro.com

PORCHER
800/359-3261
porcher-us.com

PRICE PFISTER
800/732-8238
pricepfister.com

REJUVENATION
888/401-1900
rejuvenation.com

ROHL LLC
800/777-9762
rohlhome.com

SHOWHOUSE BY MOEN
800/289-6636
showhouse.moen.com

SONOMA CAST STONE
877/283-2400
sonomastone.com

STERLING PLUMBING
800/783-7546
sterlingplumbing.com

STONE FOREST
888/682-2987
stoneforest.com

THERMASOL
800/776-0711 (West Coast)
800/631-1601 (East Coast)
thermasol.com

TOTO
888/295-8134
totousa.com

VILLEROY & BOCH
877/505-5350
villeroy-boch.com

WATERSTONE FAUCETS
888/304-0660
waterstoneco.com

WATERWORKS
800/927-2120
waterworks.com

XYLEM
866/395-8112
xylem.biz

lighting

2 THOUSAND DEGREES
847/410-4400
2thousanddegrees.com

ALCHEMY GLASS & LIGHT
323/235-6606
alchemyglass.com

ARROYO CRAFTSMAN
626/960-9411
arroyocraftsman.com

CRATE AND BARREL
800/967-6696
crateandbarrel.com

HOUSE OF ANTIQUE HARDWARE
888/223-2545
houseofantiquehardware.com

HUBBARDTON FORGE
802/468-3090
hubbardtonforge.com

KALCO
800/525-2655
kalco.com

KICHLER LIGHTING
866/558-5706
kichler.com

LBL LIGHTING
800/323-3226
lbllighting.com

MEYDA CUSTOM LIGHTING
800/222-4009
meyda.com

OMEGA TOO
510/843-3636
omegatoo.com

POTTERY BARN
888/779-5176
potterybarn.com

PROGRESS LIGHTING
864/678-1000
progresslighting.com

REJUVENATION
888/401-1900
rejuvenation.com

ROBERN
robern.com

SEA GULL LIGHTING
800/347-5483
seagulllighting.com

SHADES OF LIGHT
800/262-6612
shadesoflight.com

SHOWHOUSE BY MOEN
800/289-6636
showhouse.moen.com

THOMASVILLE LIGHTING
864/599-6000
thomasvillelighting.com

W.A.C. LIGHTING
800/526-2588
waclighting.com

tile, stone, and flooring

AMTICO INTERNATIONAL
404/267-1900
amtico.com

ANN SACKS
800/278-8453
annsacks.com

ARCHITECTURAL BRICK & TILE
317/842-2888
archbricktile.com

ARTISTIC TILE
888/698-8857
artistictile.com

CROSSVILLE, INC.
800/221-9093
crossvilleinc.com

DALTILE
800/933-8453
daltileproducts.com

LACAVA LLC
888/522-2823
lacava.com

MANNINGTON
800/482-0466
mannington.com

NEO METRO COLLECTION
800/591-9050
neo-metro.com

RENAISSANCE TILE AND BATH
404/231-9203
renaissancetileandbath.com

SHAW FLOORS
800/441-7429
shawfloors.com

SONOMA CAST STONE
877/283-2400
sonomastone.com

SPECTRA DECOR
800/550-1986
spectradecor.com

WALKER ZANGER
877/611-0199
walkerzanger.com

miscellaneous

AGAPE
agapedesign.it

ALCHEMY GLASS & LIGHT
323/235-6606
alchemyglass.com

AMEROCK CORP.
800/435-6959
amerock.com

ATLAS HOMEWARES
800/799-6755
atlashomewares.com

BALLARD DESIGNS
800/536-7551
ballarddesigns.com

CIFIAL USA
800/528-4904
cifialusa.com

CRATE AND BARREL
800/967-6696
crateandbarrel.com

CURVET USA
curvetusa.com

DANZE
877/530-3344
danze.com

ELKAY MANUFACTURING
630/574-8484
elkayusa.com

HANSGROHE
800/334-0455
hansgrohe-usa.com

HOUSE OF ANTIQUE HARDWARE
888/223-2545
houseofantiquehardware.com

HY-LITE PRODUCTS
800/655-9087
hy-lite.com

IBP GLASS BLOCK
800/932-2263
ibpglassblock.com

JACLO
800/852-3906
jaclo.com

KNAPE & VOGT
800/253-1561
knapeandvogt.com

KOHLER
800/456-4537
kohler.com

LACAVA LLC
888/522-2823
lacava.com

LIBERTY HARDWARE
800/542-3789
libertyhardware.com

MOEN
800/289-6636
moen.com

NEO METRO COLLECTION
800/591-9050
neo-metro.com

NOTTING HILL DECORATIVE HARDWARE
262/248-8890
nottinghill-usa.com

PORCHER
800/359-3261
porcher-us.com

POTTERY BARN
888/779-5176
potterybarn.com

PRICE PFISTER
800/732-8238
pricepfister.com

REJUVENATION
888/401-1900
rejuvenation.com

REV-A-SHELF
800/626-1126
rev-a-shelf.com

ROBERN
robern.com

ROHL LLC
800/777-9762
rohlhome.com

SHOWHOUSE BY MOEN
800/289-6636
showhouse.moen.com

SPECTRA DECOR
800/550-1986
spectradecor.com

THERMASOL
800/776-0711 (West Coast)
800/631-1601 (East Coast)
thermasol.com

TOP KNOBS USA
800/499-9095
800/631-1601
topknobsusa.comfg

VILLEROY & BOCH
877/505-5350
villeroy-boch.com